THE LETTERS

of

GEORGE

&

ELIZABETH
BASS

To Freya Leontine Estensen
with love

THE LETTERS

of

GEORGE

&

ELIZABETH BASS

MIRIAM ESTENSEN

ALLEN&UNWIN

First published in Australia in 2009

Copyright © Miriam Estensen 2009

Map by Ian Faulkner

All rights reserved. No part of this book may be reproduced or transmitted in any form or by any means, electronic or mechanical, including photocopying, recording or by any information storage and retrieval system, without prior permission in writing from the publisher. The *Australian Copyright Act 1968* (the Act) allows a maximum of one chapter or 10 per cent of this book, whichever is the greater, to be photocopied by any educational institution for its educational purposes provided that the educational institution (or body that administers it) has given a remuneration notice to Copyright Agency Limited (CAL) under the Act.

Allen & Unwin
83 Alexander Street
Crows Nest NSW 2065
Australia

Phone: (61 2) 8425 0100
Fax: (61 2) 9906 2218
Email: info@allenandunwin.com
Web: www.allenandunwin.com

National Library of Australia
Cataloguing-in-Publication entry:

Estensen, Miriam

The letters of George and Elizabeth Bass / Miriam Estensen.

978 1 74175 681 4

Includes index.
Bibliography.

Bass, George, 1771-1803.
Bass, George, 1771-1803 --Correspondence.
Bass, Elizabeth.
Bass, Elizabeth--Correspondence.
Explorers--Family relationships.
Australia--Discovery and exploration--British--Biography
Pacific Ocean--Discovery and exploration--British --Biography.

910.92

Typeset in 12/15 Adobe Caslon Pro and Caslon Twelve by Bookhouse, Sydney
Printed in China by Everbest Printing Co.

10 9 8 7 6 5 4 3 2 1

CONTENTS

ILLUSTRATIONS

Colour plates between pages 8 and 9

PREFACE AND ACKNOWLEDGMENTS

Exploring the oceans of the Australian and Pacific regions during the eighteenth and nineteenth centuries, British naval men sent letters home to their wives in England, some of which have survived to the present. Considered important, they were preserved by the families, sometimes for generations. The letters written by the women fared less well. Collected sporadically by men who were at sea much of the time, they more readily went astray. Some women regarded their own letters as less important than those of their husbands, and in later years destroyed them, as did Ann Flinders. Similarly James Cook's widow, Elizabeth, destroyed her letters, but, in this situation, his as well.

In the case of George and Elizabeth Bass such correspondence as was not lost at the time was preserved by members of Elizabeth's family and their descendants. We have therefore an exchange of letters written by a young couple separated by half the world after just three months of marriage. They are letters of avowed devotion, yearning, anxiety and hope, as the expected separation of eighteen months lengthened heartbreakingly into years and eventual silence. Elizabeth's letters also mirror the lives of an upper middle class English family at a time when Britain was in almost daily expectation of a Napoleonic invasion. George's letters are windows into life in England's faraway colony of New South Wales with glimpses of contacts with such diverse places as Brazil and the Pacific islands in the first years of the nineteenth century. We have, then, an unusually revealing set of letters, a tragic story of two young people with the world's oceans between them and, finally, the undoubted loss to the sea of George Bass. Short biographies of George and Elizabeth Bass briefly describe their lives before and, for Elizabeth, after the period covered by their correspondence.

The letters written to each other by George and Elizabeth Bass, which constitute the principal content of this book, are held at the Mitchell Library, State Library of New South Wales, and I gratefully acknowledge my debt to the Trustees of the State Library of New South Wales for the opportunity to publish these documents in this book. I am grateful, too, for the generous assistance of many kinds I have received at the library, with my very special thanks to Jennifer Broomhead, Martin Beckett and Mark Hildebrand, and to Paul Brunton, whose erudition provided important direction in interpreting various aspects of the story of George and Elizabeth. I am much indebted to William F. Wilson of 'Bass River' and Melbourne, for sharing with me once again his unique material on George Bass. I owe appreciation as well to the South Australian Maritime Museum; the National Maritime Museum, Sydney; the Fryer Library, University of Queensland Library; the John Oxley Library, State Library of Queensland; the Museum of London; The British Library; the National Maritime Museum, Greenwich, UK; The National Archives, Kew, Richmond; and the City of Westminster Archives, UK. Pursuing the possibility that Bass reached South America, I received valuable assistance from the Asociación de Historia Marítima y Naval Iberoamericana and the pertinent departments and staff of the Archivo General de la Nación, of Lima, Peru.

My gratitude once again to my family for encouragement and forbearance, to my editor, Rebecca Kaiser, for her always warm and enthusiastic support and to my publisher, Allen & Unwin, for the interest and cooperation that has made this book possible.

CONVERSIONS

Length

1 inch	= 2.54 centimetres
1 foot	= 30.48 centimetres
1 yard	= 0.91 metre
1 mile	= 1.61 kilometres
1 fathom	= 1.83 metres or 6 feet
1 league	= varied in different countries and periods, but usually estimated at approximately 3 miles or 5 kilometres

Weight or mass

1 ounce	= 28.3 grams
1 pound	= 454 grams
1 ton	= 1.02 tonnes

Volume

1 pint	= 0.568 litre
1 quart	= 1.1 litres
1 gallon	= 4.55 litres

Area

1 acre   = 0.4 hectare

Temperature

Fahrenheit   = $^9/_5$ degrees Centigrade + 32

Currency

1 shilling (s) = 12 pence (d)
1 pound (£) = 20 shillings
1 guinea   = from 1771, 21 shillings; not issued after 1813
1 dollar   = term generally used by English-speaking
                  people for the Spanish peseta or peso,
                  international currency at the time; the
                  peseta was issued in Spain, the peso
                  generally in Spanish American colonies.
                  In 1800 Governor King fixed the dollar's
                  sterling value in New South Wales at five
                  shillings.

Modern values for currency used in the past can only be estimated.

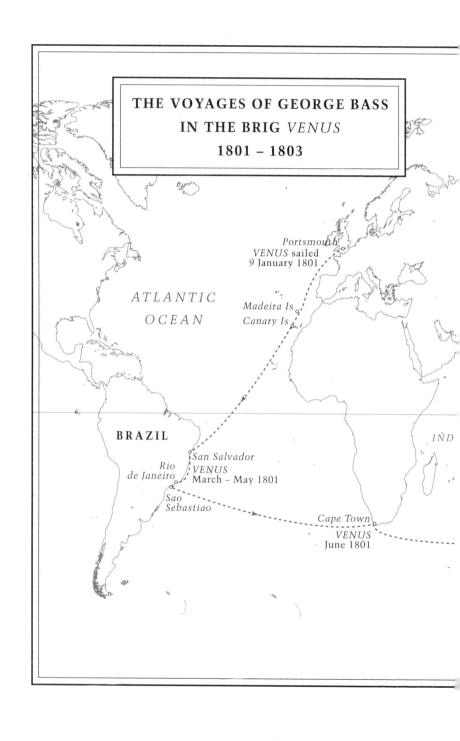

THE VOYAGES OF GEORGE BASS
IN THE BRIG *VENUS*
1801 – 1803

ATLANTIC
OCEAN

Portsmouth
VENUS sailed
9 January 1801

Madeira Is
Canary Is

BRAZIL

IND.

San Salvador
Rio *VENUS*
de Janeiro March – May 1801
Sao
Sebastiao

Cape Town
VENUS
June 1801

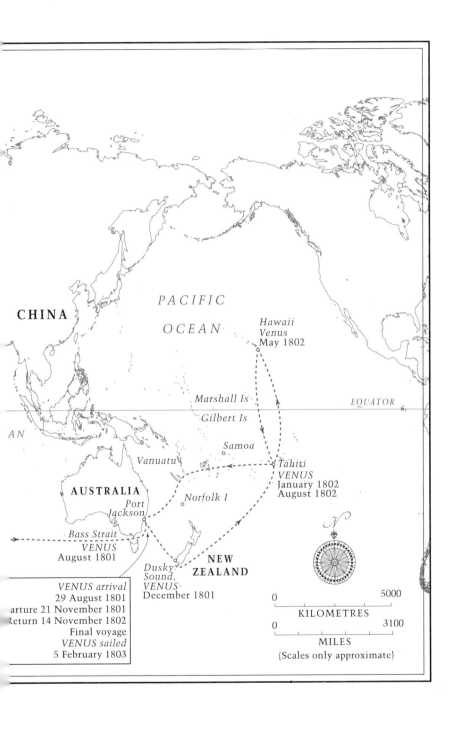

CHINA

PACIFIC

OCEAN

Hawaii
Venus
May 1802

Marshall Is

EQUATOR

Gilbert Is

AN

Samoa

Vanuatu

Tahiti
VENUS
January 1802
August 1802

AUSTRALIA

Port
Jackson

Norfolk I

Bass Strait

VENUS
August 1801

Dusky
Sound,
VENUS
December 1801

NEW
ZEALAND

VENUS arrival
29 August 1801
Departure 21 November 1801
Return 14 November 1802
Final voyage
VENUS sailed
5 February 1803

0   5000

KILOMETRES

0   3100

MILES

(Scales only approximate)

TEXTUAL REMARKS

The Bass/Waterhouse letters were secured by the State Library of New South Wales at auction on 8 April 1998. These include all known existing correspondence between George Bass and his wife Elizabeth, 22 letters written from 9 January 1801 to 19 October 1803, which in this book have been transcribed in their entirety. Each letter is headed with the names of the writer and the recipient. Date and place of writing, where given, salutations and signatures are represented as in the original. The text of each letter retains the spelling, punctuation and other details as they were written, with one exception. Abbreviations were used extensively, the omitted letters indicated with a full stop surmounted by a very small final letter of the word. Here the simpler modern apostrophe has been substituted for any omitted letters. The present location of the original letter is noted at the end of each.

An indecipherable word (or words) is indicated as such within square brackets, or a reasonable guess may be made, possibly followed by a question mark, and again enclosed in square brackets. Elizabeth Bass rarely used paragraphs in her often long letters. Some of these letters, however, have been paragraphed, although a lower case letter is preserved at the beginning of each paragraph. George Bass' paragraphing has been kept as written.

A biographical or other explanatory footnote may be inserted for persons, locations or situations which are briefly mentioned. Where individuals are more intrinsic to the narrative, the reader is referred to the Biographical notes at the beginning of the book.

To elucidate some points or to create a smooth narrative flow, the Bass letters may be linked by short paragraphs or brief quotations from other sources. The following abbreviations are used:

HRA	*Historical Records of Australia*
HRNSW	*Historical Records of New South Wales*
ML	Mitchell Library, State Library of New South Wales
TNA:PRO	The National Archives of the UK (TNA): Public Record Office (PRO)

BIOGRAPHICAL NOTES

BISHOP, CHARLES, *c.* 1765–1810, joined the British navy in his teens, but later entered the employ of a Bristol merchant, Sidenham Teast. In command of the ship *Ruby* in 1794, he sailed to the American northwest for otter furs for the Canton, now Guangzhou market, China, but results were disappointing. Heading for Hawaii for supplies, the *Ruby* was severely damaged by storms. Bishop's efforts to repair his vessel and retrieve a deteriorating financial situation took him to China and then to Amboina, today's Ambon, in the Moluccas, now Maluku, where he sold the *Ruby* and bought the brig *Nautilus*. In June 1797, with Roger Simpson on board as supercargo, Bishop again sailed for America. Unrelenting storms beset the *Nautilus*, driving her to Taiwan, Kamchatka, Hawaii and Tahiti, finally reaching Sydney. The vessel was repaired and proceeded to engage successfully in sealing in Bass

Strait. When Bishop and Simpson sailed again for China with seal skins and oil, they were accompanied by George Bass. In England in 1800, Bishop joined Bass in creating a syndicate which purchased the brig *Venus* for a commercial venture to New South Wales. In January 1801 Bass and Bishop sailed for Australia via Brazil and the Cape of Good Hope. Encountering a glutted goods market in Sydney, they headed for the Pacific islands to obtain salted pork, which was sold in Sydney. Bishop, however, was showing signs of mental instability, which, as interpreted today, was probably the onset of a bipolar disorder. In February 1803 Bass sailed alone on a second Pacific voyage, never to return. Bishop settled on a farm, but in March 1809 the lieutenant governor, Colonel William Paterson, informed the navy that Bishop was insane and a pauper confined to gaol. Arrangements were made for his return to England and he sailed from Sydney on 12 October 1809. Nothing further is known of Charles Bishop.

BLANE, SIR GILBERT, 1749–1834, was a Scottish physician who instituted important health reforms in the British navy, including improved hygiene and the use of citrus fruits to prevent scurvy. In 1783 he became physician to St Thomas' Hospital in London and physician-in-ordinary to George IV and William IV, in addition to building up a substantial private practice. Members of the Waterhouse family were among his patients, and he spoke highly of George Bass as a surgeon. He wrote *Observations* *on the Diseases of Seamen* (1785) and *Elements of Medical Logick* (1819).

DALRYMPLE, ALEXANDER, 1737–1808, was the British Admiralty's first hydrographer, 1795–1808, and a proponent of the existence of a vast undiscovered continent, the Great South Land, in the Pacific. He worked in India and the East Indies for many years promoting trade for the East India Company. Recommended by the Royal Society to lead the expedition to the South Pacific to observe the transit of Venus, he was displaced by James Cook. As hydrographer he organised the Admiralty's hydrographic department, for which he collected and published numerous important ocean charts. In 1767 he published *An Account of the Discoveries Made in the South Pacifick Ocean, Previous to 1764.*

His study of a Spanish document brought attention to the traverse by Luis Báez de Torres of the strait Dalrymple later named for him. He was dismissed from his post as hydrographer in 1808 and died shortly after.

HUNTER, JOHN, 1737–1821, was the second governor of New South Wales, 1795–1800. Entering the navy in 1754, he spent almost 30 years in active service. In 1788 he accompanied Arthur Phillip, governor of the new colony, to New South Wales, where he did valuable work surveying Port Jackson, Botany Bay and Broken Bay. In 1789 he was wrecked in HMS *Sirius* on Norfolk Island and returned to England. On the resignation of Phillip as governor of New South Wales, Hunter applied for the position, received the appointment and returned to the colony in September 1795. His governorship was fraught with difficulties. In addition to the inevitable problems of a new colony, he contended with the strong opposition of the military, who had gained control of the courts, public stores, land management and convict labour. Hunter encouraged the explorations of George Bass and Matthew Flinders and promoted zoological and botanical investigations. He returned to England in May 1801 and continued his interest in the New South Wales settlement, where in time many of his suggestions for better administration were carried out. He became vice-admiral in 1810. He died in London in 1821.

JAMISON, THOMAS, *c.* 1753–1811, arrived in New South Wales in 1788 as surgeon's mate on HMS *Sirius*. A week after the official establishment of the colony at Sydney Cove, Jamison went with Philip Gidley King and 21 settlers to found a subsidiary community on Norfolk Island. A competent and conscientious medical man, he also became active in trade, introducing George Bass to the possibilities of commercial success in a penal colony. He was in England in 1800–02, having invested £2705 in Bass' company, which made him the largest shareholder. After Bass' departure he visited the Waterhouse family, to Elizabeth's distress remarking that he would try to persuade Bass to remain in the colony to carry on more extensive trade. Returning to New South Wales, he became Surgeon

General and in time a magistrate and landowner, in 1805 being granted 1000 acres at today's Penrith. He returned to England in 1809 and died there in 1811.

KENT, WILLIAM, 1751–1812, a naval officer and nephew of Governor John Hunter, he commanded HMS *Supply* when in 1795 it accompanied HMS *Reliance* to New South Wales with Hunter, the new governor. In command of the *Supply* and subsequently HMS *Buffalo*, he made several voyages on behalf of the colony. He was a good friend of George Bass and in 1800 invested £1686 in Bass' company. In 1805 he left Australia for the last time and the following year was promoted to post captain. From 1808 he commanded the warships *Agincourt* and *Union*. The death in 1810 of his wife Eliza, who had accompanied him on several voyages, was a source of profound grief. Kent died at sea off Toulon in August 1812.

MACARTHUR, JOHN, 1767–1834, officer of the New South Wales Corps, pastoralist and public figure, arrived in New South Wales in 1790. Receiving grants of land, he built a home at Parramatta and began cultivation. His appointment as Inspector of Public Works gave him considerable power over the colony's trading community and convict labour, while as paymaster of the Corps he controlled regimental funds. His relationship with Governor John Hunter and subsequently Governor Philip Gidley King was one of virtually ongoing conflict, the various disputes culminating in a duel with Lieutenant Colonel

William Paterson, in which Paterson was wounded. Sent back to England in 1802 for trial, Macarthur interested English manufacturers in an Australian wool industry and, when remanded back to the colony, engaged in developing wool production. An instigator of the so-called Rum Rebellion against Governor William Bligh in 1808, he was exiled to England for eight years. On his return to Australia he pursued the growth of the wool industry, in the process vastly enlarging his grazing estate (60,000 acres by 1830) and becoming the dominant figure in the wool trade, as well as a member of the Legislative Council. His mind failed and he was removed from public life in 1832. He died two years later.

MOORE, THOMAS, 1762–1840, reached Sydney in 1792 but went on to New Zealand with a sealing party. He returned to Sydney and from 1796 to 1809 was the colony's master boatbuilder. In 1796 he married Rachel Turner, transported in the Second Fleet for stealing clothes from her employer. She had a son, Andrew Douglas White, born in 1793, by John White, Surgeon General of New South Wales. John White returned to England in 1795. His son, age seven, was sent to join him in 1800. Thomas Moore went on to become a major landholder (6000 acres), benefactor and active citizen of the colony. He served as magistrate in 1810, established Moore College in Liverpool and was one of the founders of the Bank of New South Wales. He died in 1840.

PATERSON, WILLIAM, 1755–1810, arrived in Sydney in 1791 as an officer of the New South Wales Corps. He took command of the Corps in 1794 and administered the colony until September 1795 when John Hunter arrived as governor. Paterson was lieutenant governor from September 1800. Interested in exploration and botany, he had visited South Africa in 1777 and in New South Wales made exploratory and plant-gathering trips into the Blue Mountains. Meeting George Bass, he seems to have inspired the young surgeon's interest in botany. He was elected Fellow of the Royal Society in 1798. In 1801 a personal quarrel with Captain John Macarthur led to a duel between the two men. The British army's Articles of War forbade duelling between officers on pain of dismissal from the service, but the practice, based on an accepted code of honour, remained. Macarthur's behaviour towards Paterson had been seen as insupportably insulting, and Paterson's only honourable recourse had been to challenge him. Paterson was wounded, but attended by Sydney's available surgeons, including George Bass, made a gradual recovery. In 1804 Paterson founded the settlement at Port Dalrymple, Van Diemen's Land (Tasmania). He embarked for England with the Corps in 1810 and died on board ship on 21 June.

WATERHOUSE, HENRY, 1770–1812, was a naval officer and the eldest son of William Waterhouse and his wife Susanna, née Brewer. He entered the navy at age twelve, under the patronage of James Luttrell, evidently related to Anne, wife of the Duke of Cumberland, and in 1786 joined HMS *Sirius* as a midshipman, taking part in the First Fleet settlement of New South Wales and Norfolk Island. He was present at the landing at Manly when Governor Arthur Phillip was speared by an Aborigine. Returning to England, he was fifth lieutenant on HMS *Bellerophon* during the English naval victory of the Glorious First of June 1794. In the same year he was promoted to the rank of commander and appointed second captain of HMS *Reliance*, which together with HMS *Supply* brought the colony's new governor, Captain John Hunter, and first captain of the *Reliance*, to Sydney, arriving in September 1795. During this journey Waterhouse became acquainted with the young explorers Matthew Flinders and George Bass. On a subsequent voyage to the Cape of Good Hope for livestock for the colony, he and Lieutenant William Kent bought 26 Spanish merino sheep, about half of which survived the stormy passage back to New South Wales. These were the first merino sheep imported into the colony. Waterhouse bought and leased several small farms, but in 1800 returned to England. He was briefly captain of HMS *Raison*, but received no further command after this. He did not marry but had an illegitimate daughter by a young convict woman, Elizabeth Barnes (or Baines), after whose death the child, Maria, was brought to England and raised by Waterhouse's family. Waterhouse was one of two witnesses at the marriage of his sister Elizabeth to George Bass, and after Bass' disappearance at sea in 1803, joined his father in trying to discover his fate. A kind and amiable man, Waterhouse made little effort in later years to secure a command. He died on 17 July 1812, possibly from illness related to alcoholism.

WILLIAMSON, JAMES, 1758–1826, served as deputy commissary and eventually magistrate in New South Wales. He profited substantially from his positions, acquiring land and livestock, including one of the largest flocks of sheep in the colony. In 1800 he invested £925 in George Bass' company, but soon afterwards sold £200 worth of his shares to William Kent. Charged with fraud in 1808, his official career in New South Wales ended. He then apparently devoted himself to farming until his death in February 1826.

WOLCOT, JOHN, 1738–1819, was a popular English satirist who, under the pseudonym of Peter Pindar, wrote a running commentary on contemporary society, government and individuals. A physician, he practised in Jamaica and Cornwall before settling in London in 1781. His verse caricatures, which included scurrilous lampoons of King George III, the author James Boswell and the artist Benjamin West, were masterful. Despite blindness in later years, he produced around 70 satirical works and some other poetry. George Bass enjoyed his witticisms, referring to the satirist in a letter to his wife. Elizabeth sought out Wolcot's works to send to George and was delighted with the opportunity to meet the author.

THE LIVES OF GEORGE AND ELIZABETH BASS

George Bass

In the early morning of 7 September 1795 two British naval ships approached the line of cliffs that guarded the entrance to Britain's Australian colony of New South Wales. Once through the gap between rocky headlands, they moved slowly past wooded promontories and white sand beaches, and by evening had dropped their anchors before the little settlement of Sydney. In the dawning light of the next morning, a young naval surgeon, George Bass, saw closely the country that would become central to the remaining eight years of his life.

George Bass was born in Lincolnshire in January 1771, when the surrounding fenlands would have been gripped in wintry greyness. On 3 February he was baptised in the centuries-old stone church of St Denis in the village of Aswarby. His father, a well-established tenant farmer,

1   *List of Those Examined and Approved Surgeons, July 1789*, from the private collection of William F. Wilson, Melbourne and 'Bass River', Victoria.

2   Ships of the Royal Navy at this time were classified, or rated, on the basis of the number of officers and the approximate number of guns they carried. These ships ranged from the huge first rates mounting 100 or more cannon on three decks to sixth rates with some 20 to 44 guns on a single deck. There were also innumerable smaller, unrated vessels, such as sloops, schooners and cutters, with varying armament.

died when the boy was six. A year later Sarah Bass moved with her son to the town of Boston. Here slate-roofed houses and narrow streets spread out from the imposing church of St Botolph with its pinnacles and tall, ornate lantern tower, and the curving course of the Witham River was lined with wharves and warehouses. The boy would have watched the plying of ships and boats on the winds and tides of the river, bearing cargoes from and to the world beyond. George was a clever, inquisitive child, fascinated by stories of the sea. Britain's sea-going traditions went back many centuries and in Bass' childhood the great 1768–79 voyages of James Cook were current news. The navy had elevated Cook to fame on the oceans of the world, and to be at sea with the possibility of making such discoveries was a prospect that gripped young George. His mother, however, had other ambitions for her only child, and apprenticed him at age sixteen to an apothecary-surgeon.

At the end of his two-year apprenticeship, George Bass travelled to London and on 2 April 1789 undertook the examinations necessary for qualification as a member of the Corporation of Surgeons. As a result he became entitled 'to the several Privileges, Franchises, and Immunities' of Examined and Approved Surgeons and to the title of Mr.[1] But the young man's eagerness to go to sea persisted, and two months later he presented himself again to the Court of Examiners, and this time received his certificate as a naval surgeon's first mate on a ship of any rate.[2] Thus on a windy day in Portsmouth in early July 1789, George

Bass, eighteen years old, boarded HMS *Flirt* and three days later saw the open sea for the first time. Clearly there was for Bass an immediate enchantment in the sight of that vastness reaching for the sky, which possessed him for the rest of his life.

George Bass had entered the practice of surgery when, like many other sciences, it was moving forward under the far-reaching intellectual impetus of the Age of Enlightenment. Generated by the great thinkers of the seventeenth and eighteenth centuries, men such as Francis Bacon, Johannes Kepler and Isaac Newton, it made fact and reason the essential features of knowledge, which was to be based on experience and observation. Such scientific thinking would shape the modern world. It would also become the basis of Bass' restless intellectual probings, his wide-ranging investigations and the application of his many talents, all of which he pursued with unrelenting energy and enthusiasm. On 4 July 1790 he qualified further, as a naval surgeon.

Bass served for five years with Britain's Channel Fleet and on Atlantic Ocean patrols. Along England's south coast the navy pursued small vessels suspected of carrying contraband and watched for French privateers waiting among craggy salients to seize British merchant ships. In late 1790 and early 1791 Bass was aboard HM Sloop *Shark*, as, in a great arc, she patrolled the North Atlantic from the Madeira Islands to the West Indies, skirting the Azores group as she steered homeward for the naval anchorage at Spithead. With the outbreak of war between Britain

and revolutionary France, the *Shark* escorted a convoy of merchant ships to Newfoundland, where she reconnoitred the coast and the islands until she sailed again for England in August 1793. Bass was then transferred to the 718-ton frigate HMS *Druid*, which cruised the Channel and the Celtic and Irish seas.

It is obvious that during these voyages Bass applied himself diligently to learning navigation and seamanship. With a crew in relatively good health, he would have had time to observe procedures, no doubt sharing in them when possible. His quick intelligence, absolute love of the sea and attractive personality would have won him the interest and friendship of others. Nor, apparently, did he neglect further study of his own craft. A list made at a later date of books owned by Bass includes volumes on both navigation and medicine, some of which he very likely acquired at this time.

In late 1793 Bass learned that the navy was fitting out two ships for a voyage to Britain's faraway colony of New South Wales on the antipodean continent generally known as Terra Australis. A new governor, Captain John Hunter, had been commissioned for the colony, founded just five years earlier, and the 394-ton square-rigged sloop *Reliance* and the 365-ton *Supply* were being surveyed and outfitted at the Deptford and Woolwich shipyards on the Thames. The prospect of adventure and exploration in a strange new land was irresistible. Bass made the necessary submission and in April 1794 was discharged from the *Druid* into HMS *Reliance*.

3 John Hunter to the Duke of Portland, 1 March 1798, HRA, Series 1, vol. II, p. 132.

4 Matthew Flinders, *A Voyage to Terra Australis; undertaken for the Purpose of Completing the Discovery of that Vast Country, and Prosecuted in the Years 1801, 1802, and 1803, in His Majesty's Ship the* Investigator, *and Subsequently in the armed Vessel* Porpoise *and* Cumberland *Schooner, with an Account of the Shipwreck of the* Porpoise, *Arrival of the* Cumberland *at Mauritius, and Imprisonment of the Commander during Six Years and a Half in that Island*, G. and W. Nicol, London, 1814, Australiana Facsimile Editions No. 37, Libraries Board of South Australia, Adelaide, 1966, vol. I, Introduction, p. xcvii.

Portrait of George Bass (1771–c.1803) c.1800, from a copy held by the Mitchell Library of an original portrait, the location of which is unknown. (Courtesy of the Mitchell Library, State Library of New South Wales)

The font in the Church of St Denis, Aswarby, where George Bass was baptised on 3 February 1771. The large stone font dates from 12th century Norman times. (Photo by David Marsden, Grantham, Linsolnshire)

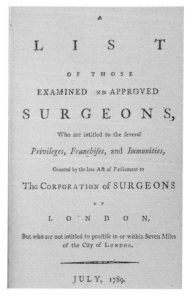

A

L I S T

OF THOSE

EXAMINED AND APPROVED

S U R G E O N S,

Who are intitled to the several

Privileges, Franchises, and *Immunities,*

Granted by the late Act of Parliament to

The CORPORATION of SURGEONS

OF

L O N D O N,

But who are not intitled to practise in or within Seven Miles
of the City of LONDON.

JULY, 1789.

List of new members of the Corporation of
Surgeons, London, April 1789, including
George Bass. (From the private collection
of William F. Wilson, Melbourne and
'Bass River')

The Thames River with Blackfriars Bridge and St Paul's Cathedral, *c.*1772, by
William Marlow (1740–1813). The arches and Doric columns, and the wherries
ferrying goods and passengers would have been a familiar sight to George Bass.
(Courtesy of the Museum of London)

BLACKFRIARS BRIDGE AND ST. PAUL'S, ABOUT 1772

St James's Church, Piccadilly, London, designed by Christopher Wren and consecrated in 1684. It was noted for the fine ornamentation of its great vaulted ceiling. George Bass and Elizabeth Waterhouse were married here on 8 October 1800. (Photo by A.K. Estensen)

Marriage licence of George Bass and Elizabeth Waterhouse. The ceremony was witnessed by Elizabeth's brother Henry and sister Maria. (From the private collection of William F. Wilson of Melbourne and 'Bass River')

F (O R)

SALE by AUCTION,

At Lloyd's Coffee-House, Cornhill,

On *Thursday* the 18th of *September*, 1800,

At Half paſt TWO preciſly,

The Good BRIG

VENUS,

CAMPBELL, Commander,

About 140 Tons Meaſurement; ſquare ſterned, with a Figure Head and ſham Galleries; built (in one of the Settlements of the Hon. Eaſt-India Company in India with Teak, ſheath'd with Wood and copper'd on it, and cheinarm'd both under the Wood and Copper agreeable to the Indian Faſhion; ſhe is double deck'd from Stem to Stern, and fitted to mount 12 Carriage Guns; her Maſts and many of her principal Yards are alſo Teak; her Stores of every Denomination are in very excellent Condition, particularly her Cables; ſhe is reported to ſail extremely faſt, and is one of the moſt compleat, handſome, and ſtrong built Ships in the River *Thames*, and will ſuit any Trade; now lying at the Swinging Chain, off *Eaſt-Lane*.

Hull, Maſts, Yards, Standing and Running Rigging, wou'd. Faults as they now lie.

INVENTORY.

ANCHORS	
1 beſt bower	1 fore ſail
1 ſmall ditto	2 ditto top ſail
	1 ditto top gallant ſail
CABLES	1 ditto royal
1 beſt bower	1 ſquare main ſail
1 ſmall ditto	1 fore and aft ditto
1 buoy rope	1 main top ſail
	1 ditto top gallant ſail
SAILS	1 ditto royal
Mr. Hooper's, Cole Stores	2 main ſtay ſail
	1 ditto top maſt ditto
1 jibb	1 middle ditto
1 foretop ſtay ſails	2 lower ſtoreing ſails
	3 topmaſt ditto
	2 top gallant ditto

Boatſwain's and Carpenter's Stores

ſome ſpare rope
ſteering ſail halliards, fore and aft
iron ſtantions, cloaths fore and aft
1 cat block
2 fiſh-hooks
6 ſcrapers
1 ſnatch block
ſundry ſpare blocks
1 tar bruſhes
1 hand lead and line

(2)

1 log line and reel	4 hhds.	3 oil jars
3 iron ſtraps, dead eyes	1 ſhook caſk	about 6 or 7 tons iron ballaſt
1 ſhip's bell	2 buckets	
hatch bars and locks complete	1 funnel	Cook and Cabin Stores
1 ſpare top maſt	1 harneſs caſk	3 camp ſtools
1 pump hook	1 tin pump	1 table
4 ditto ſpears		1 glaſs lamp
3 ditto lower boxes	Ship Chandlery	ſome knives and forks
2 pair ſcrews	4 horn lanterns	ditto diſhes and plates
ſundry carpenter's tools	1 tin ditto	1 tea kettle
6 capſton bars	1 hour glaſs	1 frying pan
1 pitch pot	1 half-hour ditto	2 tin kettles
1 ſhip's ſkeet	1 half minute ditto	1 iron hearth complete
ſome ſhot	2 braſs compaſſes	
	1 wood ditto	BOAT, at Mr. Wool's,
Cooper's Stores	2 enſign	Rotherhithe.
6 puncheons	1 jack	2 mooles
2 butts	1 pendant	4 oars

The Brig and Stores to be taken, with all Faults, as they now lie, without any Allowance for Weight, Length, Quality, or any Defects whatever.

Inventories to be had on Board, at the Place of Sale, and of

St. BARBE, GREEN and BIGNELL,

No. 33. SEETHING-LANE.

Printed prospectus offering for sale by auction the brig *Venus* on 18 September 1800. George Bass would later describe the *Venus* as being 'very sound and tight' and a 'happy little vessel'. (Courtesy of the Mitchell Library, State Library of New South Wales)

Sydney, *c.*1803, seen from the west side of the cove, watercolour, unsigned. In the middle foreground are the three hospital buildings. Across the cove are Government Wharf and on a rise, Government House. At far right, Tank Stream empties into the cove. (Courtesy of the Mitchell Library, State Library of New South Wales)

In an icy northeast wind on 16 February 1795 the ships bound for Terra Australis sailed from Plymouth Sound, initially as part of a vast 500-ship convoy, guarded from possible French attack by Admiral Lord Howe's battle fleet. Two days later the warships turned to resume their positions off the French coast, and in heavy seas and thick rain the convoy broke up, the ships heading for their various destinations.

The voyage from England to New South Wales opened what was virtually a new life for Bass. Physically and intellectually impressive, charming and gregarious, he established friendships that did much to shape his future. He became a good friend of the ship's commander, Henry Waterhouse, one day to become his brother-in-law. He evidently won the regard of New South Wales' new governor, John Hunter, who would later write of him as 'a young man of well-informed mind and an active disposition'.[3] He met Matthew Flinders, a young midshipman with dreams of adventure and discovery as vivid as his own. Flinders was deeply impressed by Bass, whose intelligence and breadth of knowledge he likened to 'a Socrates', later describing him as 'a man whose ardour for discovery was not to be repressed by any obstacles, nor deterred by danger'.[4] With high enthusiasm the two young men planned the exploration of hitherto unmapped sections of the New South Wales shoreline, insofar as their naval duties would permit. Bass was also learning the native language of the region of New South Wales to which he was going from Bennelong, an Aboriginal man brought to

5   Historians have argued the size of this boat. However, a probable
    length of nine or ten feet is indicated by a nineteenth century
    encyclopaedia of boat construction, *Tractat Om Skepps-Byggieret*
    translated by Rev. James Inman, which was originally published
    as *Architectura Navalis Mercatoria*, Holmiae, 1768, selected parts
    of which were later published in Frederik Henry as Chapman,
    Architectura Navalis Mercatoria, Coles, London, 1971.

England by the colony's former governor, Arthur Phillip, but now returning to his homeland. That Bass already had plans to make maritime excursions is suggested by his having brought on board a little boat probably some nine or ten feet in length.[5]

The colony of New South Wales, as outlined in Governor Hunter's commission, was geographically immense, incorporating nearly half of the Australian continent together with 'adjacent' islands in the Pacific. In practical terms, however, the colony occupied a narrow coastal strip roughly 20 miles in length with its principal settlement of Sydney along the shores of a sheltered cove and two smaller communities some miles inland. James Cook had charted Australia's east coast 25 years earlier, but inlets he did not enter and sections he passed by night remained unexplored.

Bass served on board the *Reliance* for over two and a half years as she made her voyages in support of the struggling colony. In early 1796 she carried supplies to the subsidiary penal settlement on Norfolk Island. In October she sailed for the Cape of Good Hope to purchase livestock, surviving terrible storms on the return journey. Nevertheless there were opportunities for exploration. With Matthew Flinders, Bass examined the Georges River and the New South Wales coast southward from Sydney to present-day Port Kembla, sailing first in Bass' little craft and subsequently in one slightly larger, both named *Tom Thumb*.

The hinterland also intrigued Bass. He participated in local excursions and in June 1796 assailed the rugged Blue

6   The mountain range was finally crossed in 1813 by well-supported expeditions led by Gregory Blaxland and William Lawson and subsequently George Evans.

Mountains to the west of Sydney, seeking to find a way across. Lack of food and water defeated him.[6] A year later he examined the seaside cliffs south of Sydney for seams of coal, returning with bags of specimens and careful descriptions of the strata, which were dispatched to England.

In December 1797, with the *Reliance* being refitted, Bass undertook a much bolder expedition. There had long been speculation as to whether the region known as Van Diemen's Land, now Tasmania, was part of the continental mainland or separated by a strait. This Bass was commissioned to investigate, for which he was given a whaleboat about 28½ feet long, a volunteer crew of six naval seamen and provisions for six weeks. Here was fulfilment for Bass' enthralment with the sea and a chance for adventure, exploration and new, hitherto unrecorded knowledge. Despite much rough weather, Bass reached and charted the deep inlet of Western Port on the now Victorian south coast before dwindling supplies and damage to the boat forced his return. He had stretched the journey over eleven weeks, and in spite of wet and often dangerous conditions, was able to deliver a sketch map and a journal of the trip to the governor. That there was a sea passage between the two bodies of land seemed almost indisputable. Then, during the months of October 1798 to January 1799, Bass and Flinders, in the little sloop *Norfolk*, finally proved the existence of a strait and completed their discovery by circumnavigating today's island state of Tasmania. Bass had further enhanced his ability as a seaman and navigator. His 46-page journal

7   Letter by 'Oceanus', *The Naval Chronicle for 1813 Containing a General and Biographical History of The Royal Navy of the United Kingdom; with a Variety of Original Papers on Nautical Subjects*, vol. XXX, Joyce Gold, London, 1813, p. 201.

was a thorough description of the trip, with numerous natural history observations and speculations. The voyage had been a high adventure and also a chance to apply his skills and intelligence to investigating and adding a fund of new information to what was known of the extraordinary continent of Terra Australis.

At this point, however, Bass could see little promise in his future. A naval surgeon was modestly paid and had no real prospects for advancement. The work had undoubtedly become routine. An unnamed contemporary wrote that Bass was 'a man possessing very great strength of mind, and of a strong robust habit, fond of enterprise, and despising danger in any shape'.[7] For such a man the career of a naval surgeon was limited indeed. Bass wanted independence, challenge and financial success. He had early recognised the unique commercial advantages of Australia's geographical position on the edge of Asia and across the Pacific from the Americas and he now saw the possible fulfilment of his ambitions in owning a ship and engaging in worldwide trade.

Bass obtained sick leave from the navy and in May 1799 quitted New South Wales, sailing to Macau on the brig *Nautilus* with Charles Bishop and Roger Simpson, two men with commercial experience in China and in the Pacific region. Bass arrived back in England on 4 August and with characteristic vigour threw himself into establishing a commercial company, selecting a ship, the 140-ton brig *Venus*, and purchasing a cargo of merchandise to be profitably sold in New South Wales and, it appears,

8   George Bass to William Waterhouse, 30 June 1801, ZML MSS 6544, ML, Sydney; also in *HRNSW*, vol. IV, ed. F.M. Bladen, Sydney, 1896, pp. 420–1.

possibly in Canton, now Guangzhou, China, for which he had received licence to trade from the monopolistic East India Company. Bass' Sydney contacts, personal friends and fellow officers, his mother and his aunt invested in his company. Charles Bishop became a partner.

Among the investors was Bass' recent commanding officer, Henry Waterhouse, at whose home, the London residence of his parents, Bass was evidently made welcome. Thus it was undoubtedly there that he met Waterhouse's sister Elizabeth. The attraction between George Bass and Elizabeth Waterhouse was clearly immediate and intense, and despite his commitment to his voyage to New South Wales, which would necessitate Elizabeth's waiting in England for his return in at least eighteen months' time, they were married on 8 October 1800. On 9 January 1801 Bass and Charles Bishop sailed from Portsmouth in the brig *Venus*. Letters now became the precious link between George and Elizabeth Bass.

After a stormy passage Bass and Bishop reached the coast of Brazil, where at the two small ports of San Salvador and São Sebastião they loaded 'Brasil goods' for New South Wales and sailed on through the South Atlantic to the Cape of Good Hope, across the Indian Ocean and through Bass Strait to Sydney. Bass wrote that the little brig was 'as deep as she can swim, and full as an egg. She turns out very sound and tight and bids fair to remain sound much longer than any of her owners.'[8]

As a commercial enterprise the voyage failed. On arrival in Sydney Bass found the limited local market glutted by

THE LETTERS OF GEORGE & ELIZABETH BASS

goods which had arrived earlier. Only food was in short supply. Thus to meet his debts and expenses Bass took his ship into the Pacific, at Tahiti and Hawaii processing a shipload of salt pork which he then sold in Sydney. The financial success of this venture encouraged him to prepare for another. It was not, however, his only intention. He had long been convinced of other economic opportunities in the Pacific area. In January 1803 he wrote to New South Wales' Governor Philip Gidley King proposing the establishment of a commercial fishery at the southern end of New Zealand, which would supply the colony of New South Wales with salt fish at a price below that of a meat ration from England. A sealing expedition was another project for which he was researching markets and prices in England. Years earlier Bass had been intrigued by the possibilities of transpacific trade with the Spanish colonies of South America. All these were enticements lying brightly on Bass' horizon when on 5 February 1803 the *Venus* cleared the Sydney Heads and sailed again into the Pacific Ocean. The *Venus* and her company of 25 men were never seen or heard from again.

As an explorer, Bass pioneered the entry into the strait that now bears his name and with Matthew Flinders proved Tasmania to be an island. He contributed to the charting of Pacific islands that now constitute parts of the ocean nations of Kiribati and the Marshall Islands. He explored the southernmost shores of New Zealand and mapped the approach to what is today Singapore.

9   George Bass to Joseph Banks, 27 May 1799, Banks Papers, Series
    72.005, ML, Sydney. Banks had sailed on Cook's first voyage and
    maintained his interest in Australia and the fledgling colony.

It was as an individual, however, that Bass was most outstanding. Gifted, versatile and avidly interested in every kind of learning, he emerges as an iconic figure in the new age of enlightenment that in the late eighteenth and early nineteenth centuries was shaping so much of the modern world. Of these cultural and intellectual developments Bass was fully aware, writing to his wife of the 'new knowledge' of which he wanted her to take advantage. People, languages, medicine, natural history, hydrography, land formations, political philosophies and any number of other topics fascinated Bass. He wrote on the anatomy of the wombat and on the habits of Australian birds. He recorded new plant life, for which he received the recognition of membership in London's Linnean Society, and discussed the possible origins of striking land formations. Perhaps unexpectedly, he was also interested in operatic music.

In this ceaseless search for information Bass applied with conviction and care the principles and methodology of science to the many disciplines which he pursued in the brief 32 years of his life. From Sydney he wrote to Sir Joseph Banks: 'I arrived here with the professed intention of exploring more of the country than any of my predecessors in the colony...'[9] This he did not accomplish, but his often strenuous efforts nevertheless produced a store of new knowledge and understandings upon which others could build in several fields of thought and activity.

Bass delighted in intellectual debate and was impatient with ignorance and with lesser minds. To his fellow surgeon

10 Thomas Jamison, naval surgeon and New South Wales entrepreneur.
(See Biographical notes.)

11 George Bass to Thomas Jamison, July 1797, in Michael Roe, 'New
Light on George Bass, Entrepreneur and Intellectual', *Journal of the
Royal Australian Historical Society*, vol. 72, Part 5, 1987, p. 252.

Thomas Jamison[10], he wrote: 'It is society, the friendly clash of opinions that brings truths to light and exalts the human intellect to the highest pitch possible.' On Norfolk Island, he said, he had found only 'the tiresome insipidity of semi-men'.[11] Matthew Flinders, who deeply admired Bass' 'knowledge and abilities', wrote of his friend's sometimes hurtful criticisms. Of Elizabeth, Bass asked that she be not only his faithful and affectionate wife, but also his 'wisest and best counsellor', an unusual desire for a man of the time. Inevitably there was a sense of isolation in being apart from so many of his peers in both intellect and the application of that intellect. Perhaps he sought to fill this void with the wide-ranging activities of his life, and possibly found a compensating sense of unconditional freedom and unlimited possibilities in the endless magic of the ocean.

Elizabeth Bass

When George Bass joined HMS *Reliance* for the journey to the colony of New South Wales, the ship's second captain, Governor Hunter being the first, was Commander Henry Waterhouse. Waterhouse's early letters home were directed to a London address in Mayfair's unpretentious Mount Street, which was lined with shops and lodging houses. By 1800, however, the Waterhouse family was residing at 29 Tichborne Street, Piccadilly, probably in a typical Georgian red-brick building of three or four storeys. Despite later references to money problems,

THE LETTERS OF GEORGE & ELIZABETH BASS

the family appears at this time to have been financially secure and socially well connected. The father, William Waterhouse, had been a page for some 24 years to Henry Frederick, Duke of Cumberland and Strathearn, brother of King George III, and Henry Waterhouse's godfather. The family probably attended nearby St James' Church, a handsome, steepled brick building evidently designed by Christopher Wren and favoured by a fashionable congregation. In 1767 William Waterhouse had married Susanna, daughter of one John Brewer, and their first child, Elizabeth, was born the following year. The family grew, and when George Bass met them there were twelve siblings and Henry Waterhouse's little daughter, Maria. Surviving letters show a close, affectionate family, in which William Waterhouse apparently played an important role as a much-loved parent.

No portrait of Elizabeth seems to exist. Remarks in letters indicate that she was petite, with Elizabeth frequently referring to herself as Bass' 'little wife'. Bass writes of her large eyes and roguish expression, and she admits that she loved to tease. She seems to have been very talkative. Bass mentions missing her 'chatter', and the family sometimes remarked on her sharp tongue, especially with regard to her younger sisters. Although they had probably known each other barely two months before they were married, it is clear that Bass was very much in love with her, and she with him.

Elizabeth would have received the education typical of a young woman of the upper middle class, which included

12 William Waterhouse to Elizabeth Bass, 9 December 1803, ZML MSS 6544, ML, Sydney.

lessons in French and music. She sang, but evidently there was no serious application to more academic subject matter. Raised in metropolitan London, she was amused by George's use of the intimate second person with the nominative 'thou', or possessive 'thy', in addressing her, evidently a country usage. She wrote in a small, neat hand, but with erratic spelling and little use of punctuation or capitalisation. Bass, to whom learning was of intense importance, urged her to improve her mind with study, and her father, an educated man, supported George. He wrote to his daughter:

> ... you know how he particularly wished you not to do any work, or what might hinder your application to improve your mind. therefore [*sic*] pray now determine to make up for lost time and agreeably surprize him and me...[12]

To Elizabeth's reply that she was too old to go to school, her father answered that it was never too late to improve and that she would have the help of books and himself, an opportunity she did not pursue. Despite their many errors, her letters reflect dignity, warmth and courage, and profound love for her husband.

On 8 October 1800, George Bass and Elizabeth Waterhouse were married in St James' Church, Piccadilly, standing beneath the magnificently vaulted and panelled ceiling, around them the glint of the church's numerous brass candlesticks. Their witnesses were Elizabeth's sister

13 Probably Henry Waterhouse's young daughter. (See 'Waterhouse, Henry', Biographical notes.)
14 George Bass to William Waterhouse, 8 October 1800, and Henry Waterhouse to William Waterhouse, undated, on the same sheet, ZML MSS 6544, ML, Sydney.

Maria and brother Henry. The ceremony was conducted by the curate J. Maddy.

A special licence secured by Bass from the Archbishop of Canterbury had evidently precluded the necessity of publishing banns. On half-pay from the navy, and with all he possessed invested in preparations for a speculative commercial venture to distant New South Wales, Bass was obviously uncertain of Elizabeth's parents' reaction to the marriage. Thus, it was not until after the ceremony that Bass sat down and in a large, firm hand, wrote to William Waterhouse:

> Dear Sir,
> Your daughter Elizabeth and myself were this day married at St James's Church. May it be an increase of happiness to us both, as well as to our friends. Pray present my most kind compliments to Mrs. Waterhouse and kind remembrance to Miss Maria[13] and believe me to be yours truly in friendship,
> Geo. Bass
> My wife requests me to present her love and duty but she cannot write herself. Elizth. Bass.[14]

Henry turned over the sheet of paper and wrote:

> My Dr Father,
> You will certainly think me an impudent fellow when I inform you I this day gave irrevocably away your daughter formerly Eliz. W— now E. Bass.

15 George Bass to William Waterhouse, 8 October 1800, and Henry
    Waterhouse to William Waterhouse, undated, on the same sheet,
    ZML MSS 6544, ML, Sydney.

My long knowledge of the worth of Mr Bass to whom she has united herself makes me congratulate you & my Mother on the occasion—of my own concerns I can say nothing.

Yours affectionately,

HWaterhouse[15]

The immediate reaction of Elizabeth's parents is not recorded, but it is clear that George Bass was accepted warmly into the Waterhouse family. To this Bass responded with loyalty and affection, habitually referring to Elizabeth's siblings as his brothers and sisters.

The young couple moved into Bass' upper floor lodgings in Arundel Street, The Strand. Developed over a century before by the Earl of Arundel to raise money for the construction of a new town house on the Thames, it was a narrow street that ran steeply down from the busy thoroughfare of The Strand to steps descending to the river's edge.

Without pause Bass continued the intense activity of preparations for the voyage to New South Wales. Thousands of items of merchandise were bought and packed into the *Venus*. Bass' mother, Sarah, came to London, returning to Lincoln as Bass' sailing time approached. With preparations for the voyage complete, Elizabeth accompanied her husband aboard the *Venus*, sailing from the Thames into the Channel to the great naval anchorage of Spithead at Portsmouth. Accommodation for Elizabeth and George was found with a Mrs Dozells at Gun Wharf in nearby Portsea as the *Venus* joined the ships of the East India convoy, a

THE LETTERS OF GEORGE & ELIZABETH BASS

large assemblage of vessels waiting for favourable winds to be escorted into the Atlantic under navy protection. On 9 January the wind shifted, and George took leave of his wife. Somehow Elizabeth managed to hold back her tears but then, watching as a harbour boat carried George to the ships and out of sight, she gave way to feeling utterly abandoned. A final note from George, brought back to her by the boatman, redoubled the anguished reality of their separation. The convoy sailed, and a few days later split up, the ships steering for their various destinations. In extremely rough weather, Bass crossed the Atlantic to the Brazilian ports of San Salvador and São Sebastião, from where he sent letters to Elizabeth, the first of which she received exactly seven months from the day of his departure.

Not until it was certain that changing winds would not force the convoy to return to Spithead did Elizabeth leave her lodgings, spend some time with friends and then return to the family home in London. Except for brief, occasional visits elsewhere, Elizabeth remained there, writing to Bass and awaiting his letters. Her position in society as a young married woman without her husband at her side was difficult. The necessary propriety of her conduct had clearly been a subject of discussion between George and Elizabeth before his departure. On a more personal level there was the fact that they had known each other perhaps no more than two months before they were married, and were married only three months before they were parted. Despite the deep devotion between them, concerns did arise, as is clear from their letters.

Confronted in New South Wales by financial difficulties, Bass voyaged to South Pacific islands for saleable salt provisions for the colony. In February 1803 he sailed again into the Pacific. Then month followed month without word or sighting of his ship. Gradually, as his failure to return to Sydney was noted in the colony, and Elizabeth's letters went unanswered, his disappearance became increasingly evident. William and Henry Waterhouse traced every possible lead in seeking word of him, and Elizabeth refused to accept that he was dead. In January 1806, however, Bass' friend William Kent apparently certified for the Admiralty his disappearance at sea. Elizabeth seems to have finally acknowledged her loss and, probably in the face of her father's declining fortunes, applied for a naval widow's pension. She received £40 a year, backdated to 1 July 1803. Privately, however, she appears to have always considered herself not a widow, but a wife awaiting her husband's return.

By June 1811 financial difficulties seem to have forced the removal of the Waterhouse family from Tichborne Street to 6 Smith Square, Westminster, and at some point Elizabeth took lodgings of her own in nearby Marsham Street. In the next few years she suffered the loss of her brother Henry, her mother and, in 1822, her beloved father. Elizabeth Bass died in 1824 and was buried with other members of her family at St John's Cemetery, Westminster.

THE LETTERS

On 9 January 1801 the wind shifted to a direction favourable for the sailing of the great assemblage of ships that waited at Portsmouth's Spithead anchorage, and seemed to be holding long enough to carry the convoy out of the Channel. Amid the rush of getting his ship underway, George Bass scratched out a note to his wife, which he sent ashore by one of the little wherries plying the harbour to deliver goods and messages.

George Bass to Elizabeth Bass

Venus, Jan 9 1801

My dear Bess

I have no cash to entrust to your care. and have only time to say God bless you my love. Remember

16 George Bass to Elizabeth Bass, 9 January 1801, ZML MSS 6544, ML, Sydney.

me to our father [William Waterhouse] most
kindly Adieu adieu
    Yours most affect'ly
    Geo Bass[16]

It was the first missive in the three-year correspondence that with many losses and delays would make its fitful way halfway around the world to and from George and Elizabeth Bass.

Communication between Australia and Britain depended on such ships as from time to time made the many-month journey to the other side of the globe. Letters, including government reports and official documents, were entrusted to persons travelling in the direction of the letters' destination, sometimes being passed several times from hand to hand or ship to ship. That many were lost is evident from references made in surviving correspondence to questions that had received no response. Some of Bass' letters to his London agent were among these, as were letters to his wife and from her to him. Under the circumstances it became usual to share one's letters with the friends or family of the writer. Elizabeth's father comments on the failure to arrive of letters sent to him and to his son Henry by Bass from Brazil. However, Bass' friend, Lieutenant William Kent, who had received his, showed it to William Waterhouse, so in Waterhouse's words 'it was the same thing'. For a young wife of three months, however, it was clearly not 'the same thing'.

17 Evidently Maria Innes, eldest daughter of the Innes family who were long-time friends of George Bass. Elizabeth misspells the Innes name repeatedly in her letters.

18 Mrs Maseals is not identified.

19 Captain Savage and the pictures are not explained.

20 A Captain Mattley was commander of HMS *Hindostan* sailing from the Cape of Good Hope for England in early 1802. The reference is probably to his family living in the Portsmouth area.

21 James Innes, HMS *Vigilant*, had for twelve years been a friend of Bass, who was regarded by the Innes family as one of their own. Bass was evidently the godfather of one of the Innes daughters. James Innes invested £150 in Bass' company and witnessed the signatures of Bass and Bishop on the Articles of Agreement which spelled out their rights and obligations as partners. After Bass' departure the family warmly befriended Elizabeth. Later Bass' library, brought to England by Thomas Jamison, was left with the Inneses until it could be retrieved by Bass on his return to England.

22 Mrs Bennet, wife of a naval officer.

23 Lodgings occupied by the Basses at Gun Wharf in Portsea while the *Venus* awaited departure.

Elizabeth Bass to George Bass

St Georges Square Januy 28th 1801

My ever Dear George
How shall I discribe my feelings when you left me
I had stifled my Tears that I might not distress
you it seems as if I had lost every friend I had in
the World, I watched the Boat till it was quite out
of sight when the Waterman [boatman] brought
your little Note and last. Then I felt redoubled
our cruel seperation like I told you I was shure
you would not return that Night I had flattered
my self you would. Miss Inice[17] came to me but I
insisted on her keeping an ingagement she had to
Dine and spend [word indecipherable] with Mrs
Maseals[18] Captain Savage called to let you know
he had left the Pictures[19] he promised you at
Mattleys[20] when he found you were gone he said
he was D[rest of word indecipherable] sorry for
it but would bring them to me in the Evening in
case I should have an oportunity to send them but
I have never seen him since. Mr Mrs Inice[21] and
Mrs Bennet[22] to my great relief came to me early
in the Evening indeed they showd every mark of
friendship that was possible wished me much to
go home with them. I refused wishing to stay at
Mrs. Dozells[23] till there was no probibility of
your return.

24 James Innes was storekeeper for French prisoners of war kept on ships at Portsea. In his letters Innes mentions that there were thousands of prisoners.
25 Alexander Dalrymple, the British Admiralty's first hydrographer, 1795–1808. (See Biographical notes.)

poor Mr Inice was in great distress when he found you were intirely gone as he left his party on purpose to render himself of every assistance in his power, he could not come to you according to his promis on account of his being obliged to take in a great number of French Prisoners[24] he ast me what you said I unfortunately said you thought he had taken a Glass of Grog too much and had forgot the promis he had made poor fellow his distress was beyond discription at the Ide that you should for a moment supose it neglect when it was merely Business and so far from haveing taken too much he had drank nothing but table Beer the hole Day. Mrs Inice and Bennet said they would clear him there as they never saw him soberer in their lives. and beged I would inform you that he had formed a resolution the first Day of the Year to leave it intirely off and never has been in Liquor since. he beged I would inform you that nothing in the World could hurt him more than his dear friend George Bass leaving England with such an opinion of him.

O my dear George how I watched the Weather Cock not from a selfish wish to see you again, indeed I could Ill bear another parting. but the Day after you left me I received a parcel of Charts from Mr. Delrumple[25] you so much wished for, and another the following Day. O I would have given Thousands if I had them to have got them

26 Henry Waterhouse, naval officer. (See Biographical notes.)

27* ibid.

28 Rear Admiral Sir Roger Curtis, 1746–1816, Commander-in-chief of the British naval squadron at the Cape of Good Hope.

29 The Palmers mentioned were probably related to John Palmer, Commissary-General of New South Wales, 1790–1810, whom Bass knew well. He was in England from 1794, returning to the colony in 1800 with his wife, two sisters and a brother, but other relatives probably remained in England.

30 *Nutwell*, evidently a naval vessel not otherwise identified.

31 Lindegreens, seemingly an agent for naval officers.

32 Henry Waterhouse, naval officer. (See Biographical notes.)

33 James Sykes, George Bass' agent, Arundel Street, The Strand, London.

34 On 8 January, the day before he sailed, George Bass wrote to his mother, leaving the letter with Elizabeth. She added a description of George's departure before posting it.

conveyed to you as it constantly dwelt on my mind that having them might save your dear Life. I wrote to my Brother[26] and beged he would go to Mr. Delrumple and say I had them in my possesion and beged to know if I might send them by the first Ship bound directly for the Cape. Henry[27] wrote by return of Post to say he had been and and [*sic*] that Mr. D had given leave beged I would have them ready to send out at a moments warning and adress them to the care of Sir Roger Curtis[28] as the Commanding oficer then to let him know what steps I had taken and he would write with them to Sir Roger. Mr C Palmer[29] wrote me a Note Yesterday to say the Nutwell[30] was come round and would sail in three Days and if I sent them to Lindegreens[31] Ofice to Day they would send them, God send they may reach you and may be as much service as I wish them. I wrote to Henry[32] Yesterday to beg he would send me the letter he promised to go with them. all the Letters you left with me I made a Parcel of and sent by the Coach to my Father except the large sealed Packet and the Letters with the Government Bill these I hope to deliver my self but beged my Father would inform Mr Sykes[33] I had them in my possesion he has done so and likewise delivered all the London Letters and put the rest in the Post. I filled up the one to your Mother[34] and have had an answer from her, she is very well but not pleased at not haveing

35 HMS *Mars* was a 74-gun two-decker.

it sooner I did not like to send them till the third
Day after you left me in case you should return.
O how I long to hear that you are perfectly well
and Happy. I went the Wednesday after you left
me to Miss Palmers they had called several times
to claim the promis we had made of my going to
spend some time with them (they where much
disapointed at not knowing the time you went as
they wished to send Letters and a trifle of their
deceased sisters as a remembrance they behaved
in the kindest manner possible to me wished much
I would spend some Months with them but I only
intended staying a Week,

I was very unwell when you left me and
continued getting worse Saturday the 17th Mrs
Benet and Inice called on me to know when I
intended coming to them just at that time I was
taken with a Violent shivering Mrs I saw imediately
what was the matter with me and wished much to
take me home with her Miss P [Palmer] being all
Young people but it was too late I was obliged to
go to Bed and was taken in the same way as in
Arundle Street, fortunately Doctor Culling Surgeon
of the Mars[35] was on a Visit to Miss P (before he
went in the Navy he practiced nothing but
Midwiferey for twenty Years in Gloucestershire)
therefore I feel in very good hands he attended me
very kindly and gave me Tincture of Roses which
prevented its coming to so Violent a pitch as in

36 What Sarah Bass wrote in her pocket book is not mentioned again, but presumably it related to hopes for Elizabeth's pregnancy.

37 Napoleon's victorious campaigns in Italy and Germany were bringing about peace negotiations between France and the continental powers. Britain, alone against France, remained on a war footing.

Arundle Street. still I fear I shall be obliged to ask
your Mother to scratch out what she wrote in her
Pocket Book. O my dear George it will hurt me
more than I can discribe being obliged to disapoint
your hopes.[36] Mrs. Inice spoke to a Doctor
Waymouth about [me] he kindly ofered to attend
me but as Doctor Culling was there Mrs I declined
it. Miss P paid me every attention in their power
and thank God I am better in Health than I have
been some time tho very weak I did not come to
Mrs Inice till Monday Evening as Doctor C did
not think it proper for me to go out fearing a
relapse Mrs Inice Bennet and Family are as kind
as they possibly can be to me. for the first time
since you left me I walked a little way Yesterday
with Mrs. Bennet they say I shall go every Day as
I felt better after it. Mr. I is on Board as there is
an order from the Admiralty that every Oficer and
Man are to sleep on board their Ships and on no
account to have leave of absence they tell me the
Streets are quite deserted at Night.[37]

I have had very kind Letters from my Father
Henry and Sisters beging I would come home.
Henry wished to come down to me, but I beged
he would not as every one is kind to me O how
severely I felt your loss while I lay Ill, I had no kind
Husband to sooth me and call me his dear little
Wife. I had only to lay and think of all that was past
and the thousand little things I might have done

38 Elizabeth's conduct as a young wife away from her husband, and consequently her reputation, were, as was typical of the period, of serious concern to them both.

39 Charles Bishop had become almost a member of the family and during Sarah Bass' stay in London appears to have been referred to teasingly as her husband. (See Biographical notes.)

for you I had neglected indeed my dear George I often think I might have made you happier than I did. if ever we meet again rest ashured I will neglect nothing that lies in my power to make the rest of your Life as happy as you can wish. God send it may be but 18 Months instead of three long Years. Mrs. Inice says the soonest she will part with me will be in a Fortnight indeed they are very kind to me but all places are alike. I can receive no pleasure and hate to go out, still I am better here till I find my self strong enough to take the Journey [to London], be ashured my Conduct here or where ever I may be shall be such that George Bass shall never Blush to own his little Wife[38] now my dear I must forget the past and look forward to the many happy Years I hope we have to come every Day will shorten our cruel seperation that you may meet with every success and happiness you coud frame an Ide of is the sincere wish of your Afectionate Wife Eliz'th Bass

P.S. Comp'ts to Captain Bishop or Charles your Mother wrote to him but it could not arrive till after you started she beged I would send to the Post ofice for it as it was filled with nonsense to her Husband.[39] I did so but there was no such letter there.

P.S. Mrs Inice Bennet and Family desire their best Comp'ts as does the Palmers pray my dear George

40 Elizabeth's comment evidently related to the League of Armed Neutrality formed at the end of 1800 by the principal Baltic states, notably Russia, with Sweden, Denmark and Prussia, against Britain. The League was broken up by Nelson's victory at Copenhagen on 2 April 1801 and changes in Russian foreign policy following the death of Tsar Paul I in March.

41 HMS *Ramilies* was a third rate, carrying 74 guns on two gun decks.

42 Elizabeth Bass to George Bass, St Georges Square, 28 January 1801, ZML MSS 6544, ML, Sydney.

do not let any oportunity be lost even if it is only a little note to say I am [well] will be the greatest pleasure I can receive in this Life, O how happy I should be if I was certain the Charts and this Scrawl would ever be in your possesion if you can read it you must excuse it as I have written it in a great hurry. just dined am desired by Mrs. I Bennet Maria Catherine and Isabella to give their Loves. it is generally suposed we are going to War with the Russians Danes and Sweeds[40] as all the Shipping is to be got ready as fast as possiable. the Gentleman that attended me is removed from the Mars to the Ramilese[41] in Harbour. I have no more to say but God bless you ten Thousand blessings attend you
  Adieu Adieu[42]

At the beginning of March a stormy crossing had brought the *Venus* to the Brazilian coast.

George Bass to Elizabeth Bass

Venus at Saint Salvador, Coast of Brasil
Mar. 8. 1801

I intend in this letter to write only a few words to my beloved Betsy another and a better opportunity than the ship which brings this will offer itself before we leave this port.

43 Commodore of the convoy's naval escort, George Stewart, Lord Garlies, later eighth Earl of Galloway.
44 A miniature portrait of Elizabeth.

We are arrived here all safe after a passage of 45 days from the <u>spot where we parted</u>, that is, my dear Bess, you and I.

The wind became so unfavourable to the progress of the fleet a few hours after we left Portsmouth that I doubt not but that you were led to expect we should return. Oh no! the perseverance of Lord Garlies[43] overcame every obstacle, very much to the temporary inconvenience of poor Venus as well as to several other vessels in the fleet.

I was unable, my love, to answer the little scrap you sent me off by the waterman at Spithead, for just as he came alongside the signal was just thrown out for the fleet to make all sail and we were every soul of us fully engaged.

I have preserved your little scrap. <u>Little Bess</u>[44] is well, I look at her <u>now and then</u>; she hangs up over the foot of my bed, and looks quite roguish let the winds blow high or low, even the excessive heat of st Salvador are not able to put waggery out of her countenance. Adieu little Bess; adieu. adieu to her original!!

Pray write to me at China, write several letters; open all your soul to me; tell me all that grieves you, all that delights you. Yes, my <u>Bess Bass</u>, <u>I will</u> return; return to you, and that as speedily as possible.

The India House is the place in London where your letters must be sent and let them be directed

45 Philip Gidley King, governor of New South Wales 1800–06.
46 George Bass to Elizabeth Bass, 8 March 1801, ZML MSS 6544, ML, Sydney.

to Robr. Berry Esq at Canton. or if to me on board the brig Venus there it may be sufficient.

Write also to me at Port Jackson to the care of Govr. King[45], for we shall return to that place from China. Offer my kind love to our sisters and never forget that you fully posses my esteem & affec' love

G Bass[46]

This letter was the first received by Elizabeth from George after his departure from England. It reached her precisely seven months from the day of their parting.

George Bass to Elizabeth Bass

Venus St Salvador Coast of Brasil
March 18th 1801

My beloved Betsy, this is my second letter to thee. What can I have to say but to repeat what I had already said. To tell thee of love is to talk nonsense to thee; thou must be well assured of my love.

To tell thee that I recollect with pleasure that we have passed a few happy weeks together, will be unnecessary because I trust thy feelings are like mine. Oh Bess; may nothing prevent a renewal of those short lived happy days!

47 A chip hat was a fashionable wide-brimmed hat.

This is the first time we have parted my Bess, and if fortune is kind to me in my first undertaking I will have a ship for my next that shall be big enough to hold both thee and me. I often wish thou wast with me and as often am rejoiced that thou feelest none of the inconveniences of our crowded but happy, little vessel. I want to say much but I can say nothing to thee; nay I would even hazard some advice although my dear Bess has too much good sense and is too well acquainted with the world to stand in need of any.

My soul flies towards thee when I cast my eyes upon a heap of chip hats[47] that lie before me exposed for sale; one of them resembles a white hat my Bess used to wear.

Oh Bess there is no people like the english people and amongst them I love thee most! Oh Bess we ought to be, we must be, surely, shall be happy with each other again.

Write to me a long, very long letter, open thy soul, pour upon the paper rough as it arises, thy hopes thy fears, thy joys, place thyself before me let me see my honest Bess.

Adieu, my love adieu. Address to me in the care of Govr King at Port Jackson to the care of Robr Berry Esq. at Canton or on board the Venus there to be left at the English factory till her arrival. Present my warmest wishes to all our dear friends amongst whom thou art living, and ever look up to me as

48 George Bass to Elizabeth Bass, 18 March 1801, ZML MSS 6544, ML, Sydney.

49 On separating from the convoy out of Plymouth Sound, the *Venus* was assailed by fierce gales but for some eleven or twelve days managed to keep company with HMS *Hussar*, a 38-gun frigate. Dropping behind off Spain's Cape Finisterre, the *Venus* crossed the Atlantic alone. By April the *Hussar* had returned to England, without hoped-for letters for Elizabeth. Henry Waterhouse, however, was able to secure an official report of a brig of *Venus'* description sighted off Madeira, heading south.

50 Mr Embank, evidently a naval surgeon.

a man by whom thou never shall be deceived. Be happy, be happy Geo Bass Bishop's love to you & all your house. I had nearly forgotten[48]

Elizabeth Bass to George Bass

Tichborne Street April 25th 1801

My Dear George
My Father who is always as kind as is possible to me took a very long letter in the City yesterday for me to go by Captain Flinders who expects to sail either the 3rd or 10th of next Month he saw one of the Pursers of the China Ships who told him they had taken leave and there would be no other go till the latter end of the Year and that if I had Letters they must come this Morning. I would not miss the opportunity but it must be very short. my dear George you will see by my last I am disappointed in all my hopes. The Hussar[49] returned and no Letters for your poor Bess. I have been Ill for some Months. pleased my self with the hope there was a little one on the Road that would be able to call you Father on your return but in that I am disappointed I always felt the same as in Arundle Street still there were causes to contradict it.

on the 15th I was very Ill sent for Mr. Embank[50] he ordered An exercise Rosemary Tea a Draught

THE LETTERS OF GEORGE & ELIZABETH BASS

to take twice a Day and Port Wine he has promised
to take care of my Health during your absence and
sais you must do the same by Mrs. E on your
return if he is absent. I am now so much better I
scarcely know my self. my Spirits are very low.
how should they be otherways no Letters can be
expected from you for some Months. nay I know
not even weather you are living God forbid I
should be a Widow in reallity O my dear dear
George I know not weather, change of seen &
Countries has made you forget your little Wife,
but I give you my word you are never out of my
Thoughts. I am shure I Love you better than ever.
I did not think I should feel the seperation so
cruely believe me all the World is nothing to me
without you. if ever we meet again, and there is
room for you there must be for me I never will
give my concent to be parted again. (you used to
say great talkers do the least do you see) believe
me I am sincere. Captain Flinders has been Married
a Week they came to London on Thursday he
called for my Letters offered to do anything in his
power for me either at home or Abroad says he
was sorry their stay in London would be so short
it was intirely out of his power to introduce Mrs.
F. to [me] that he much wished it, with all my
Heart I wish them happy, they have every prospect
of being so as he has it in his power to take her
out with him they can share each others Cares and

51 Matthew Flinders' plan to bring his wife with him on his voyage of exploration to Australia did not materialise. Told by the Admiralty that by doing so he would probably lose command of the expedition, he sailed without her. Deeply disappointed, Ann Flinders returned to her parents' home in Partney, Lincolnshire.

52 Peter Pindar was the pseudonym of John Wolcot (1738–1819), a writer of satirical verse on English politics, society and individuals. Bass obviously enjoyed his witticisms. (See 'Wolcot, John', Biographical notes.)

53 Arthur Phillip, first governor of New South Wales, under whom Henry Waterhouse had served in the First Fleet and in the new colony. Phillips remained a good friend of the Waterhouse family.

pleasures.[51] we can do neither O George you have not been gone quite 4 Months I feel it as many Years. pray write to me every oportunity that will be the greatest pleasure I can now receive

I should have sent you all the Newspapers but they tell me it is of no use unless you had been on a station. I got my Father to inquire for the new Publications he can hear of but two that he thinks will please you one of which he bought for me Yesterday called Crimes of Cabinets. the other he is going to get to Day if he can, he could not get it any more Yesterday. I believe it is called out of Office it is Peter Pinders[52] last Publication if he can get it he will send it with the other by Captain Flinders there is something more of his comeing out if I have an oportunity will send them to New South Wales. O how I wish I could know weather there is anything you want I could send you what pleasure I should do it with. we herd from my Brother Henry Yesterday, he has been at Admiral Phillips[53] these two Months had a very bad Fit there is perfectly recovered and had intirely left of Grog only drinks Wine and Ale he is now at Portsmouth intends Staying a Week he tells me the Charts are not gone yet. I believe there is a heavy spel laid on them it seems as if you never was to have them, but now I suppose if they are sent they will be of little use by the time you can get them.

54 HMS *Hindostan* was a 54-gun naval vessel; the *Nutwell* was
   evidently also a navy ship.
55 *Venus* was a popular name for ships. In an 1804 listing of Royal
   Navy vessels there were two Venuses. A whaler by that name is
   mentioned carrying letters to Bass.
56 Young William Waterhouse was living in Spalding, Lincolnshire,
   apparently engaged in the coal business.
57 HMS *Hussar*, with which the *Venus* had at first kept company
   after sailing from Plymouth Sound on 9 January 1801. The *Hussar*
   returned to England in April.
58 The Norvills were friends of Bass, Bishop and the
   Waterhouses.

this is either the 6 or 7 Letter I have written the first by the Nutwell either two or three by the Hindostane[54] to the Cape one by the Venus[55] to New South Wales one by C't Flinders and this to China. perhaps you may never get any of them. I hope your mind is too employed to feel the want of them as I do. your Mother and me keep up a regular corespondance she desires her Love [sent to you] says her reason for not Writing is that I can always let you know how she is and that she has nothing more to say than her prayers for your safety and speedy return most Heartily I join mine with them she has had the Gout in her right Arm and left Foot when I herd about a fortnight since it was in both her Feet. otherwise she is in good health and tolerably comfortable I had a letter from my Brother William[56] (he writes to me most Weeks I cannot say I answer them as often as I ought) he begs for God's sake I will write to him imediately he says do I suppose he had neither feeling for me or my Husband. he has herd long since of the arrival of the Hussar[57] but I have never let him know any paticulars. all I know my self is that I was most cruely disappointed and Mrs Norvil[58] who is very kind sent every Day to Laids [word indecipherable] for me all she could learn was that you parted Company on the 20th of January in a Gale of Wind in the Bay of Biscay. O wish I knew more my self

59 Clarkes and Creseys (Cresseys), evidently family friends but not otherwise identified.
60 Elizabeth Bass to George Bass, 25 April 1801, ZML MSS 6544, ML, Sydney.
61 The year should be 1801.

in my last I told you I had been at Mrs Clarkes & Creseys[59] for a call they behaved very kind to me. I very seldom go out when I do my Father goes with me he is my only Beau my dear George believe me your little Wife lives for you alone that God almighty may grant you Health prosperity a safe Voyage and speedy return is the Prayer of you truely affectionate Wife Eliz'th Bass

P S my Father Mother Brothers and Sisters joins me in Love. best Comp'ts to Captain Bishop [tho?] I fear you will hardly be able to read my scrawl but indeed I never was so much huried as to get it in time my dear Father is going with it in the City Adieu Adieu[60]

As Bass had instructed, Elizabeth sent some of her letters to Canton (now Guangzhou), China. As he never reached China himself, what letters so addressed he eventually received can only be surmised.

George Bass to Elizabeth Bass

Venus [Island of St Sebastian] April 27th 1800[61]

I write to you my beloved Betsy; but great must be our luck if it ever reaches you. These false, deceitful Portuguese may never send onwards my ardent

62 George Bass to Elizabeth Bass, 27 April 1801, ZML MSS 6544,
    ML, Sydney.
63 George, in fact, wrote three letters to Elizabeth from Brazil.

wishes for thy health and happiness. We are all well, and are on the point of quitting, to go on direct for Cape Good Hope, a little, paltry place, the Island of St. Sebastian some 10 score miles westward of Rio Janheiro. We have been here 23 days. Came in for wood and water. I will write to thee by the first conveyance from the Cape. My kind Love to thy father and all thy family. Let me be retained in thy memory as I deserve thy faithful

Geo Bass[62]

George Bass to Elizabeth Bass

Venus Cape Good Hope June 30 1801

And now my dear, my beloved, wife I resume the delightful employment of addressing thee. Twice[63] I wrote to thee from Brasil and told thee how dear thou art to me. I had prepared a very long letter for thee which upon reflection I have destroyed for, I believe, this selfish reason, that I would bring thee before me a second time. In the abstract I will tell thee what it contained for I almost repent my selfish folly.

I earnestly and by every endearing tie besought thee to labour at the improvement of thy mind, that thou living in the midst of civilised society and in a country fruitful in new knowledge make

THE LETTERS OF GEORGE & ELIZABETH BASS

thyself able to instruct me upon my return from my wild uncivilised voyage, and by the new brilliansy of thy mental endowments add strength to the powerful cement that lies, I trust, already between us. Make thy self my wisest and best counsellor, as well as my faithful, affectionate wife. Remember my Bess you have a husband who will not forsake you nor ever cease to love you as long as my Bess remains deserving of it.

I think my love this voyage once done we shall then have a fair chance of living together the remainder of our days. Not on shore Bess for I fear we must beat the wave in company and seek our bread on many & distant shores. Hard lot for thee! but thou mayest be happy even under such circumstances. Neglect not thy french nor thy music I w'd recommend several modes of improvement to thee and particularise them but leaving thee as I have done without the means of procuring the necessary sources from w'e [wherever] they are to be drawn I feel my self constrained to be silent and must leave thee to the guidance of thine own internal rectitude and distinction between the probable and improbable means of preserving thy happiness and my love. I will return to thee my dear Bess but there is yet a long round voyage to make, & much to be done. Write to me at Port Jackson to the care of Gov' King. some ships are now here that sailed from England in March. I had no letters by them.

64 George Bass to Elizabeth Bass, 30 June 1801, ZML MSS 6544, ML, Sydney.
65 Margate, on the Kent coast south of the Thames estuary, was a popular bathing resort town due to its sandy beaches. A variety of other entertainments also drew summer visitors.

Remember me kindly to our sisters and believe thy
affectionate and anxiously waiting Geo Bass[64]

This letter reflects vividly the importance Bass attached
to intelligence and education and something of the sense
of isolation felt by a man who frequently found himself
intellectually above his peers. Now he wanted to find in
his wife his 'wisest and best counsellor'. Deeply as Bass
loved his Bess, her willingness to learn and her mental
accomplishments would be to some extent a part of his
regard. On his voyage Bass had brought with him the works
of Mary Wollstonecraft, the dedicated feminist advocate
of social and educational equality for women. Unusually
for a man of the time, Bass clearly believed that women
could achieve much more intellectually than was generally
accepted. Yet he was fair. He had left her. He would not
be there to guide her efforts. Therefore he destroyed the
letter evidently detailing what he expected of her and now
left it to her to determine the 'probable and improbable' of
what she could accomplish. The letter made clear one other
important point: Bass saw their future tied to the sea.

Elizabeth Bass to George Bass

Margate[65] August 1801

My Dear George
Sunday 9th I was made as hapy as I can be while
you are absent, I received the first Letter from you

66 The Downs was an area off the coast of Kent employed as an anchorage for merchant ships awaiting favourable winds to take them down the Channel or up the Thames. It was also an anchorage for naval ships and the base and headquarters of the North Sea Fleet.

67 James Innes, naval officer. (See notes 21 and 24.)

since you left me dated 8th of March St Salvador
O my love I felt more than I can discribe, you was
well, wrote in good spirits, and had not forgot
your little Wife, be ashured my dear you have
never been out of my thoughts a moment since we
parted, and I must be wonderfully changed if you
ever are. I will own I have been a self tormentor,
you had been gone just seven Months, to the Day
I read your Letter, sometimes I fancied you was
laying in a French Prison, at others Ill, and worst
of all an ever dear Husband friend and Protector
lost to me for ever. but thank God, you was safe,
well and in good spirits, this has taken a heavy
load off mine; I am in Hourly expectation of
another from the Brasils. and others from the Cape,
as the East India Ships, now lay at the Downs[66],
if they bring me as favourable a Letter as the last
I ought to consider my self a happy Woman. still
my dear George I hope they will bring me better
news. it seems you have been constantly tormented,
in the first place bad Winds (I hoped but could
not expect you back as Mr. Innis[67] told me the
Wind was fair for three Weeks) second and most
of all the great danger and anxiety, you must have
been in from the Rat hole, of all the Animels I have
seen or herd of they were, my greatest dread, and
in this case would have been my death or what is
worse deprived me of my sences, for Life, for
believe me my Love when I ashure you on my

THE LETTERS OF GEORGE & ELIZABETH BASS

honour, if you had been lost, your little Wife
would have been so too, as my feelings could never
support the severe Shock. but there shurely is a
little Cherub aloft to preserve the life of my dear
George, and send him safe home to me never to
part more till our great Master calls us, as the next
Voyage I will go. your fate shall be mine. I shall
be able to bare hardship and dangers with you and
if we go to the bottom, of what consequence is it,
we go together, and leave no helpless Children
behind us. I fear your health must have suffered
from anxiety and fatigue, it was but very indifferent
when you left me, tho you endeavoured to conceal
it from me, and I am shure you have had nothing
to make it better; I know after you got safe to St
Salvador, finding the town stocked would hurt
you. and I am told you will meet with the same at
the Cape, and Port Jackson, but pray for my sake
do not let; these things hurt you, I am shure you
will do you best, and believe me when I ashure
you if you return with only a bare support, I shall
be as happy to receive you as if you possed
[possessed] all the wealth of the Indies even if you
have lost all, you are still in the Navy and are
esteemed very cleaver in your Profession.

you say you have preserved my little scrap, I
am shure it was not worth it, but I know not what
it contained, my Heart was too full. I wish I could
take Little Besses place, if it was but for one Hour,

68 Rear Admiral Sir Roger Curtis, naval commander at Cape Town.
69 Alexander Dalrymple. (See Biographical notes.)
70 Presumably the Spice Islands, i.e. Moluccas (now Maluku).

you would see my Countenance brighter than ever
you saw it, if you gave me but one smile, but that
is denied me for a long time, my George you have
been gone but Seven Months yet, O how long the
time seems, and I fear I have little hope now of
seeing you in Eighteen Months, as all these
disapointments, must detain you longer than you
expected, I am sorry for it but it cannot be helped.
I can only pray that we may have a happy meeting
at last. you beg I will write to you at China, I sent
one Letter by the ships for that place the 25 of
April directed to the care of Robt Berry Esqr my
Father put it in the India House for me and will
send this and more, as I see by the Papers the Ships
are taken up for China. this is the 12 Letter I have
written you since you went but I fear you will get
few of them, as I did not know it was necessary to
adress them to the care of any one at Port Jackson.
those to the Cape were to the care of Sir Roger
Curtis[68], likewise the Charts from Mr. Delrumple[69]
which I much fear would not get there till after
you had left. I would have given all the world if I
had possesed it, for you to put back as one parcel
came the Day you left me, and the other the next
with a Letter desiring you would examin the
Charts, before you went for the Nutmegs[70], as there
are dangerious Rocks (I sent the Letter with them)
God send you may escape them and pray be
cautious of the Saviges that Murdered one

71 Incidents that involved the killing and in some cases the eating of European landing parties on Pacific islands are well documented.
72 This letter appears not to have survived. Whether Bass received it is a further question.
73 Thomas Jamison, naval surgeon. (See Biographical notes.)
74 Jamison had left a wife and son and seemingly a daughter in England when joining the First Fleet for New South Wales.

Surgeon[71], remember you do not stand alone in
the World, you have a little Wife that cannot say
how much she loves you.

you desire me to tell you all that Grieves me
and all that delights me. my Father and family are
kind to me, I have nothing particular to Grieve me
but your absence, and the uncertainty of your fate,
nothing to delight me till your return. the greatest
pleasure I have received since you left me, is your
kind Letter and the promis you make me of
returning to me as soon as you can; as I have not
been quite easy on that head, in my last[72], I told
you Mr. Jamison[73] let a Word slip which he wished
to recall as soon as he saw it hurt me, but he should
have considered, I was no Baby or quite a Fool, he
turned too quick. He sayd he was very sorry you
had left England before he came, but as that was
the case he should go out again to persuade you
to stay in that Country, a term of Years, to carry
on a trade from there to different places, as soon
as he saw it hurt me he sayd, he should do every
thing in his power to assist you and get you home
as soon as he possiably could, as he had suffered
enough himself from a seperation.[74] I conceive had
Mr Jamison been at Port Jackson when you got
there he might of been of great service but I know
of none he can be on your return, except to make
me a miserable Woman by detaining you. but I am
shure you have too much Love for me to be detained

75 William Waterhouse, brother of Elizabeth.
76 Jack Waterhouse, evidently Elizabeth's youngest brother.
77 The Pearsons, friends of the Waterhouse family.

by any one longer than is absolutely necessary, come and fetch me and then it will be a matter of indifference where we go or stay, I have now my dear George Bass opened all my Soul to you and told you what has grieved & pleased me most. your Mother has written to my sister Mary since I have been here, she was very well except for a little of the Gout. as soon as I had red your Letter I wrote to her and gave her all the Heads, I could not of my Fathers [letter] as they did not send it from the Post office till my Letter was gone, but I supose it is of no consequence, as I hope you wrote to her. I wrote likewise to my Brother Henry, William[75], Mrs. Innis, and my Sisters I told you in my last, my Father and Jack[76] were here with me, my Mother came to us last Week, it is a delightful place, plenty of amusements, that while you are away I cannot enjoy therefore do not go. all I like is to walk by the Sea side and on the Cliff every thing here is very dear and it will cost me much more than I wished, but my Love I will not ruin you. good by God help and prosper you

Your Truely Affectionate Wife Eliz'th Bass

P S I forgot to say we have been here 5 Weeks my sisters wrote me word, Mr. and Mrs. Pearson[77] drank tea in Tichborne Street about a Fortnight since, they called with the intention of taking me down with them but the Bird was flown I had a

78 Presumably the Waterhouse family business, which is not described. In a letter to Elizabeth her father remarked that Bass did not want her involved in the business so she might devote her time to improving her education.

79 Roger Simpson sailed with Charles Bishop on the brig *Nautilus* as 'trader and factor'. When Bass joined the *Nautilus* on its final voyage to Macau and Canton (Guangzhou), he and Simpson charted some of the islands presently parts of the Gilbert (Kiribati) and Marshall archipelagos. (See 'Bishop, Charles', Biographical notes).

Letter from my friend Mrs Munsey of Hereford
last week, as kind as ever tho from my neglect of
her I did not deserve it. she says as I say I have
nothing to do with the Business[78] and have been
Ill, she would advise me to come to Hereford as
it would be of service to my Health, and that I
might, depend on them all, making it as comfortable
as lies in their power. and as I know the way of
Business they are in am shure I would put up with
the inconvenience attending it, but all they can say
is that they should be very happy to see me, hopes
I have rec'd the long wished for Paquet from my
Dear Husband, (yes my George I have but it is
but one Letter yet) and that you are well and will
return a Nabob for both our sakes is [paper torn;
their?] sincere wish. it is not mine, for they [the
Nabobs] ingeneral have more Sins to answer for
than I hope my [paper torn] will ever have, but her
meaning was good she is a kind hearted Woman,
and always was very fond of me. her Letter pleased
me very much,

we have made a slight aquaintance with a
Gentleman and Lady, that lodge, in the next House
to us I find she is a first Cousin of Mr. Simpsons[79],
that was with you in the Nautiless, she begs if you
see Mr S you will tell him her Name was Louisa
Bird his first Cousin, that she has Maried a Mr.
Funnour Linen Draper in Four St Meerefields
[Mirfield?]. she has three as fine Children as I ever

80 Elizabeth Bass to George Bass, Margate, August 1801, ZML
    MSS 6544, ML, Sydney.

saw (I almost envy her they are very fond of me) and is going home next week to bring another begs her Love to her Cousin should he [you] happen to hear from him. she saw his Mother about three Weeks since she was very well. my paper being full Adieu Adieu my Love

Margate my reason for comeing here, was a wish to be with my Father who is always very kind to me and to be out of the confined House in London. but it will be more expence than I expected I have promised to pay half the Lodgings as well as many other things I wish to do, I have followed your advice, have nothing to do with the Business, put out my Washing and many other little things, that make me in a great measure indipendant and much happier than I should have been otherwise, if any one ofends me I tell them I have a Husband and am independant, all this my Love you desired, I only hope you will not think me extravegent in comeing here, I am as careful as I can be here, and indeed I should not have felt so comfortable without my Father you told me to open all my soul and I have done so ten thousand blessings attend you Eliz't Bass[80]

Elizabeth's distress on hearing Thomas Jamison say he would persuade Bass to remain in New South Wales longer than intended was enough for her father to comment in his letter to George: 'Betsy is rather alarmed by Mr. Jamison

81 William Waterhouse to George Bass, 19 August 1801, ZML MSS 6544, ML, Sydney.

82 Elizabeth's letter of 21 February 1801 appears to be lost.

having said he will use his influence with you to remain in that country...' Waterhouse went on to say that he had assured his daughter that this would not be so. He added that time until Bass' return was not going fast enough for 'Betsy, who wishes to annihilate a year or two'.[81]

Elizabeth's remarks on her independence make it clear that she and George had discussed her position as a married woman without her husband and also her limited finances. Her income would have been half of Bass' naval half-pay of less than five shillings per day, the other quarter going to his mother. However, ensconced with her family, Elizabeth was obviously comfortable. The family business to which she refers is not explained.

The *Venus* arrived in Sydney on 19 August 1801 and Bass wrote to Elizabeth and to his father-in-law, William Waterhouse, letters that were dated 3 and 4 October, evidently when the opportunity to dispatch them arose.

George Bass to Elizabeth Bass

Venus Port Jackson Oct 3, 1801

My beloved Bess.
I have received thy letter, its length pleased me) of Feb 21.[82] I have told your father all our commercial concerns and therefore thou wilt learn from their complexion that our voyage must be long, very long. So then Bess its a miss! is it.

83 *Tant pis*—so much the worse, too bad; *tant mieux*—so much the better.

84 'The Walls' probably refers to Portsmouth's old harbour wall by the so-called Round Tower. It offered a view of the sea and of ships coming in and out of the harbour. The letter in which Elizabeth describes this sad and lonely walk was probably that of 21 February.

85 John Palmer, 1760–1833, first Commissary-General of New South Wales, arrived in the colony with the First Fleet. Palmer engaged extensively in farming, milling and as a small ship owner in coastal transport. In 1801 he built a home then considered very luxurious. Sophy (or Sophia) was one of his several children. This and other references to the Palmers suggest that members of the family were particular friends of George and Elizabeth Bass.

Robert Campbell, 1769–1846, a partner of the Calcutta firm of Campbell, Clark & Co., established himself in Sydney, engaging in trade, construction and colonial administration. In 1825 he became a member of the first Legislative Council of New South Wales and later was one of the first settlers in the district where Canberra was later built. He married Sophy Palmer in 1801.

86 Elizabeth's younger sisters.

Tant pis if our voyage goes well tant mieux if it goes bad.[83] I'm in a gloomy mood Bess. I wish I had thee with me, but thou must wait at home till I fetch thee, w'ch shall be as soon as possible, for I long to have thy chatter. We will not part anymore. Thou shalt put on trousers and sought it out all over the world with me, but then thou must promise to make no third person for us. And so my Bess thou went to the Walls[84] and the sea looked gloomy, and the little brig was not there. My love thou were then but young in thy widowhood. Recollections were yet strong upon thy mind. I am extremely happy that thou wert satisfied with thy stay at our friend Innes's. They are kind and worthy people. The Ladies here make many inquiries after you (Mrs. King & Patterson) and desire to be kindly remembered to you. They regret much you are not here. Sophy Palmer is married to a Mr Campbell[85], a bengal merchant established here in trade. I shall write to thee again very shortly and send it by a better and I think quicker conveyance.

Write to me at all opportunities. Be assured my affection for thee is firm and sure. Since we could not add to the cement by living together let us at least do it by frequent correspondence.

Adieu my love adieu, say kind things to the girls[86] and do Bess take pains with thy spelling

87 George Bass to Elizabeth Bass, 3 October 1801, ZML MSS
6544, ML, Sydney.

for thou dost stick in and take out parts of thy
words without law or licence
> Your affectionate husband
> Geo Bass[87]

George Bass to Elizabeth Bass

Port Jackson Oct'b 20th 1801

I wrote to thee, my beloved Bess, a few days since
by an Indian conveyance; one by Cape Gd Hope
now offers and I must not withhold from telling
thee we are all well. In a few weeks another Cape
conveyance will occur and I shall then write thee
a longer letter and also write to my other friends,
but thou hast claims upon me that admit not of
my losing any opportunity however vague &
uncertain it may be.

In my last I told thee of the bad markets we
have found here. This state of things has induced
me to enter into a contract with Govr King to fetch
salted pork from the South Sea Islands & we are
now mustering casks and making every preparation
for fulfilling our contract as speedily as possible.
But my love all this protracts, most cruelly
protracts, our voyage. Necessity, however, leaves
us without an appeal. It must be so! There is no
other way to bringing our voyage to a profitable

88 Henry Waterhouse, naval officer. (See Biographical notes.)

89 'Have been out together', fought a duel.

90 On 14 September 1801 Lieutenant Colonel William Paterson and Captain John Macarthur, both officers of the New South Wales Corps, fought a duel in which Paterson was wounded. Macarthur left Sydney in November 1801 to be tried in England. Bass' remarks reflect his view that Macarthur was a troublemaker. (See 'Paterson, William' and 'Macarthur, John', Biographical notes.)

91 Captain Neil McKellar, who had been Paterson's second in the duel, was ordered to England, carrying Macarthur's sword and Governor King's dispatches on the conflict. He sailed from Sydney on 29 March 1803 in the 103-ton American schooner *Caroline*, which disappeared at sea.

92 William Waterhouse, brother of Elizabeth Bass.

93 George Bass to Elizabeth Bass, 20 October 1801, ZML MSS 6544, ML, Sydney.

conclusion. Tell Waterhouse[88] that Capt. McArthur will shortly sail for England in the Porpoise under arrest. He is sent home to add or rather to restore peace to this country. He & Col. Paterson have been out together[89]; the latter was wounded in the arm the first shot but is recovering fast.[90] So much for colonial news but tell him [Henry Waterhouse] was I to relate to him all the particular circumstances of the Colony at present I w'd fill a quire. He will soon see McArthur and MacKellar.[91] My kindest love I beg to your father & mother & to those saucy girls your sisters not forgetting our bro in Lincolnsh.[92] Adieu adieu my love Geo Bass[93]

Elizabeth Bass to George Bass

Tichborne Street Nov'r 9th 1801

My Dear George
I rec'd your second Letter from Brasil the 23th of September you may easily supose the pleasure it gave me to hear you was well and so warmly express your Love and affection for your poor little Wife. I have been lamenting my self with a Thousand fears for your safty. my time passes as usual walking on the Cliff and Rocks [at Margate], thinking of you and looking back with pleasure, on the short but happy time we spent

THE LETTERS OF GEORGE & ELIZABETH BASS

together, O my George my Love when shall we
be happy with each other again most heartily I
pray that nothing may hapen to prevent it. you
tell me if you are successful you will have a Ship
big enough to hold us both the next Voyage, God
send you may be, but weather you are or not, the
same room that holds you must do for me, as I
never can give my concent to another parting, it
cannot it must not be, I shall be happy to share
your fate let it be what it will you say you often
wish I was with you indeed my Love I always
wish it. how pleased I am you find it a happy little
Vessel, that my George will be of some comfort
to you. but pray are you all turned Quakers, for
from the Thees and Thous in your Letters to me
it seems you are compleately so. well if you are I
dont care, you are still George Bass and I shall
never find any one I can Love so well. you dont
know how much you have made me value my
little Chip Hat by remembering it particularly
as it is the one I was Married in, I have had it
died black.

my George I want longer Letters what success
you meet with, a discription of the places you go
too, what sort of Ladies you meet with (that I may
be acquainted with the places and People I am to
see) inshort everything that happens to you till
our happy meeting. O my dear George I often set
and think, with what pleasure we shall meet each

94 A sauce made from the juice of mushrooms.
95 See note 76.

other, my Sister Mary declares she will have the first Kiss, but I will not alow it, as I posetively will not spare you a Moment. but O how many and anctious Months must I pass before I shall see that happy Day

as we were walking on the Cliffs about the latter end of September on the side of a Field we saw some Musherooms, this led to a farther search, the Field was large and contained a great many, I am very fond of them and of gathering them, from that time till our leaving Margate, my Father and me spent all our time in getting them (our Evenings ingeneral at the Play) we eat them every Day as well as having made 4 gallons of Catchup.[94] with a melancoly pleasure I remembered the 8 of October, you was far from me my George but that Day twelve Months I became your Wife I was determined to keep it as well as I could, asked the only friend we had there (Mrs. Stewart) to come and spend the Evening with us, she declined it her Daughters being Ill but beged we would go there I went home Dined off Stewed Mushrooms & Fish, Father Mother Jack[95] and myself went there to drink tea, we had just began when Mrs. S said I was very dull and ought to be merry on my Wedding Day, I said I felt uncommonly Ill in a moment a faintness swiming in the Head and cold shivering seized me, I had just time to get out of the Room before I was taken with a Violent

96 See note 76.

97 Evidently travel between London and Margate was commonly done by boat. The Nore, in the Thames estuary, was a heavily used anchorage for both naval and merchant ships.

Vomiting, I wondered my Father (who is always kind) did not come to me, but on my return to the Room found he had been just in the same state we got home as well as we could and continued in this state three Days, inshort we were Poisoned from the Mushrooms having staid in a Brass sauspan till they were cold, thank God we recovered but had a very narrow escape, how would my George have felt if he herd that on the Day twelve Months he was Married his Wife and Father was Poisoned, and Dead. as soon as we got well we continued gathering Mushrooms till we left Margate October the 24th, very Rough weather, we had scarcely cleared the Pier before almost every soul on board was Sick your poor little Wife one of the first such a Vessal I believe never was seen I had one Sick at my Back one in my lap and Jack[96] in my Shoes, so we continued till we passed the Nore, but as you see by this we are safe at home again.[97]

the Day after we arrived I had a letter from your Mother and she begs I will thank you for your kind Letter, and hopes you will continue to write to her when ever an opertunity offers you have her best wishes, she thinks she shall now live till your return, as she has had her health better this Month past than it had been for a considerable time. October the 27th I read your dear letter from the Cape, O my George it gave me pleasure and

98   Thomas Jamison, naval surgeon. (See Biographical notes.)
99   George Johnston, 1764–1823, New South Wales Corps officer
     and landholder. Arrested on several charges and sent to England
     for court-martial in late 1800; the trial was squashed and he
     returned to the colony in 1802.
100 William Kent, naval officer. (See Biographical notes.)
101 James Williamson, public servant in New South Wales. (See
     Biographical notes.)

pain Your stay from every account is lengthened that was a cruel intelegance, but cannot be helped I fondly hoped you would be home in Eighteen Months I am cruely disapointed, but it cannot be helped your Voyage must be performed. I have only to beg and intreat, you will take care of your self for my sake, as remember my future happiness depends on it, if not my existence and that you will let no one persuade you to stay Abroad longer than you have compleated this Voyage. as I told you before I am ready to go where ever you please, but if you stay and leave me you make me a miserable Woman for life, Mr Jimison[98] & Major Johnson[99] for instance are going out again, Mr Kent[100] and Williamson[101] are going I strongly suspect they wish to detain you but you have a Wife, that love you most sincerely and thàt most earnestly beg you will not neglet and stay from her. but I know you too well you will not let interest get the better of Love and affection. My George why did you distroy the letter you had written do you supose I could be tired of reading any thing from you. you wish me to improve my Mind I will do my best, but I am ill able to do anything now you are away, as to giving instructions, I must always look to you for that, in French and Music I will try to improve my self, but do not expect much of me, depend on it you will find me ever an afectionate and faithful Wife and firmly yours

102 Maria Innes. (See note 17.)
103 Mr Bennet, naval officer and friend of Innes and Bass.
104 Bass owned some 90 books on a wide range of topics, including
     medicine, navigation, foreign languages, philosophy, and Greek
     and Latin classics. The books apparently never reached Elizabeth
     and there seems to be no record of what eventually became
     of them.
105 George Johnston, army officer and New South Wales landholder.
     (See note 99.)

I had a letter from Maria Innis[102] last Week they are all well and Mrs I begs I will begin to prepare for your next Voyage as she says you will not go with out me (you may be shure that pleased me) Mrs Bennet has been to Plymouth to see Mr B[103], was with him but three Days, this is all she has seen of him since you left, but they are in Daly expectation of the Ships comeing in Port, but there is no such happiness for me. Mr. Jimison left all your books in Mr. Innises care, I wished to have had them home but it seems Mr. Jimison thought they would not be worth the Carrage by land, therefore must wait there till an oportunity offers, on your return.[104]

O my George how much I was hurt to find you had not received my Letters, could you supose for a moment I would neglect you or let any ships go without Letters, I wrote three in February, and one or two by the Ships in March & sent the Charts, from Mr. Delrumple, many an anctious hour it has cost me your not haveing them, as from the letter that came with them, I know they were of the utmost consequence to you, they were all adressed to the care of Sir Roger Curtis. my Brother Henry asked Major Johnstone[105], if they go to the Cape to get them all and take them to you to port Jackson God knows weather you will ever get any of my Letters this is the 16 I have written. I own I should have thought you very cruel, if I had, had

106 John Hunter, governor of New South Wales 1795–1800. (See Biographical notes.)

107 Arthur Phillip, 1738–1814, first governor of New South Wales. Henry Waterhouse sailed under him in HMS *Sirius* of the First Fleet.

108 The Pearsons, evidently close friends of the Waterhouses.

109 Apparently a mutual friend of Elizabeth and Mrs. Offray.

110 Henry Waterhouse, naval officer. (See Biographical notes.)

no Letters. Mr. Kent lent my Father his Letter to show me, he seems much pleased with your Voyage, has got two Hundred of Mr Williamsons share [in the *Venus*], he likewise red his Letters to my Father, I was out, the Governor H[106] brought me his Letter to read. Admiral Phylip[107] has called several times, always inquires very kindly after you and desires to be remembered. Mrs Pearson[108] Drank Tea at our House on Friday they are all well beg to be remembered, wish me to spend some time with them at Christmas, I believe they are going on very well. I had a Letter the Week before last from an old friend, from Hamburg Mrs Offray scolding me for letting Mrs Cased[109] be the first to inform her of my mariage (as before she left England she beged I would let her know when ever it was likely, to take place) she inclosed two Yards of Black Lace Value about 5 Guineys to make me a Cap, it pleased me much as it was kind and the first preasant any friend had made me since I have been you Wife. I had a very kind letter from Mrs Munsey of Hereford beging I would go and spend part of my time with her during your, absence but it is too far and too expencive and I find wile I was at Margate I missed Writing by the last ships, there was not time to let me know. but Henry[110] wrote, he is very kind to me always offering me Money, but as yet I have not wanted it, being Peace I supose he will have no Ship. he is

111   Lymington, a port town across The Solent from the Isle of Wight.

112   Prize money resulted from the sale of a captured enemy ship, the money divided according to a strict scale among the officers and crew who took part in her capture. This particular prize money apparently resulted from several vessels having been declared prizes in Plymouth as the result of an embargo when Waterhouse was there as captain of the *Reliance*. The amount of Waterhouse's share was complicated by Governor Hunter's also being ranked as captain of the *Reliance*.

113   James Sykes, George Bass' agent, Arundel Street, The Strand, London.

114   The Thomases, naval friends.

115   The Clives referred to were Edward Clive, Baron Clive (later Earl of Powis), and his wife, Lady Henrietta Antonia. Edward Clive, son of Robert Clive who established British power in India, served from 1798 to 1803 as governor of Madras. His wife appears to have preceded him home to England in early November 1801. Evidently Mr Thomas and Captain Brown were members of the Clives' respective retinues.

116   ibid.

117   William Kent, naval officer. (See Biographical notes.)

118   Elizabeth Bass to George Bass, 9 November 1801, ZML MSS 6544, ML, Sydney.

now with us, talks of going to Portsmouth, to
Morrow, from there to Limington[111], I wish he
would get Married and settle, I think he would
make a very good Husband we are inhopes he will
get the Prize Money.[112] Mr Sykes[113] has got yours,
twenty Pounds, Eleven Shillings, I wish I knew
what you would wish to have done with it. we must
fix on something, they asked my Father weather
it was to be devided between our Mother at Lincoln
& me, I shall write and ask her, as on my return
from Portsmouth I sent her a Five pound Note,
she returned it with a kind Letter, saying that while
she had the half of your half Pay she could always
lay by at the Years end some Pounds, but at any
rate if they will let me have it I shall take it from
there they told my Father the half Pay would be
received as last Wednesday, but he has been too
Ill ever since with a Bowel complaint to go for
mine. Mrs Thomas[114] I supose is made a happy
Woman Mr T returned last Week with Lady
Clive[115], I have not seen her since, Captain Brown
will not return till Lord Clive[116] does. my Brother
William is still at Spalding, intends writing to you
by Mr Kent[117], and will be very happy to hear from
you if you will write to him pray let me know at
what time you think it likely you will return. all
our family beg their Love, good by God bless and
prosper you my dear George. Your Afectionate
Wife Eliz'th Bass[118]

119   Bass does not explain this enigmatic sentence. It is clear, however, that Bass' active mind was already at work on some project that was more adventurous than salting pork.

George Bass to Elizabeth Bass

Venus Port Jackson Nov 12, 1801

I have written to thee my much beloved Bess twice already from this place, and have now but little to tell thee, except to repeat my assurances of love.

Oh my Bess this untoward outset of our voyage throws all my plans of expected speedy return very uncertain.

We are now upon the point of sailing to the S. Sea Islands for pork for government. This adventure is a certain gain & has no speculation in it. We think it will clear all our Debts in London and so rid us of all troubles on that head, & put the first great obstacle aside. Governor King is just recovered from a very severe fit of the gout. His death wd. have been but little lamented here.

Tell your father a chilling gloom hangs over our immediate prospects, but we see some very cheering rays of sunshine break through in places, that promise the succession of a burning day. A peace with Spain after our return from this pork business wd. make matters better than ever. If no peace [and] war shd. then have taken place a few vigorous and wary exertions will make all go well.[119]

We arrived in this part of the world upon the top of a general glut. Happy for us that we can

120 Thomas Moore, from 1796 to 1809, was Sydney's master boatbuilder and subsequently a major landholder. (See Biographical notes.) He married Rachel Turner, transported with the Second Fleet. She had a son, Andrew Douglas White, by John White, Surgeon General of New South Wales.

121 George Bass to Elizabeth Bass, 12 November 1801, ZML MSS 6544, ML, Sydney.

find a gainful employment for our vessel and be waiting until the glut begins to take off.

While we are gone for pork the most saleable part of our cargo will be left with Mr Moore[120] the husband of little Andrews mother.

Remember my most kind love and compliments to your mother & father and those dear little girls your sisters, to Bros H. & W. & J.

Adieu my love adieu

Geo. Bass[121]

Elizabeth Bass to George Bass

Tichborne Street December 15th 1801

My Dear George

O how slow the time passes, you have been gone little more than Eleven Months, and to me it seems as many Years, the weather is so cold I can hardly hold my Pen, altho I have made a Fire in my little Room to write this by, this time last year my dear George I was confined to my Room but I was happy I had a dear Husband to set beside me comfort me and make me forget I suffered pain. with pleasure I look back to the time I used to get on the Chair Kiss and take leave of you, then anctiously wait the well known Voice on the Stairs of all I held most dear, a thousand things nay all every thing that

122 Bass may have spoken of some of his wider ranging ideas for trade. Charles Bishop had experience in sealing on the northwest coast of America and this may have been discussed as a possibility. On arriving in Sydney and finding no market for his English merchandise, Bass considered sealing.

passed between us is fresh in my memory. O what
pleasure I felt when you returned unexpectedly and
Dined with me at Deptford, last Christmas Day
we Dined alone these are the two happiest Days I
ever remember to have spent. your poor Bess always
wished to be alone with you, but seldom had that
wish gratified. now she cannot even hear from you
for a great length of time, O my Love how I dread
the hardships and dangers you will suffer, that horid
place you are to pass in going to get the Nutmegs.
(O my George pray for my sake remember the fate
of the last Surgeon that ventured there, you canot
be too cautious and must check your bold
Interprizing Spirit) and the severely cold and dreary
Winter on the Nor West Coast of America.[122] God
I trust and hope will guard and give you strength
to go through all you desire I will open my Heart
to you, then forget my scrawl appears nonsence to
you as it does to me, as one moments consideration
would have told me you would have passed all these
hardships long before you can receive this. but you
must excuse me I feel restless and uneasy your fate
is uncertain, you are very very far from me the
Winter is cold, I miss you indeed my George I do,
I am always wishing that circumstances had not
obliged you to leave me, or that I could have shared
your fate my dear Father and Family are kind to
me, I go out but seldom when I do I receive no
pleasure, I can attend to nothing you wished me

123 The Cresseys were family friends.
124 While in Sydney, Captain Gardiner of the whaler *Venus* had shared a house with Charles Bishop.

inshort I am always seeking for something I cannot find, that is a much loved and dear Husband at any rate if not improved you will find me what you left me always in thought and deed truely and affectionately Yours. I had a letter from our Mother at Lincoln Yesterday she is tolerably well begs her love, says she has written and directed it to you at China, she is much hurt at having no Letter from you from the Cape, in all my Letters I have indeavoured to persuade her the Letter had mised but she says she is certain you never wrote to her or it would have come with the rest.

Young Mr Cressey[123] brought Captain Gardner[124] to see me the 24th of November you may easily conceive the pleasure it gave me to hear when you Dined with him you was in good Spirits and grown Lusty and looked very well. let me beg that you will fatiegue yourself as little as possiable and not let disapointments hurt your spirits all your friend are well ashured you will do your best and know you cannot forsee what may happen, you know my George you injured your health strength and Spirits very much before you went by over Fatiegue and anxiety, I am shure I neither expect or wish for more than will support us comfortably, and that I well know cannot be gained [without] this Voyage (I wish it could) I shall be willing and happy to accompany you in your next, as I can never bear another parting, I always read your three Letters

125 Evidently a member of Sykes' staff.

with pleasure, particularly, the part in which you ashure me you will return to me and that as speedily as possiable. as I have long had my fears that some of your friends wished to detain you at Port Jackson, and that the hope of making your fortune might induce you to do so, but on reflection I am shure you have too good a Heart to let any consideration, make you, neglect your poor little Wife, and make her miserable. I often think with what pleasure we shall meet, God send nothing may happen to prevent it, there must not there shurely will not be. but O there is yet a great length of time before that happy Day comes. my Father went with me the 8th of this Month to Mr Sykes, it being long past the time, they promised to send me word when they had received the half pay I thought your leave of absence must be nearly out and they might forget to make aplication, Mr S told me they had intirely forgot, to send for your Money, but would the first Wednesday next Month, but would pay me then, I received the half of the half pay and prize Money twenty one pounds to gether, the same they promised to send your Mother, I asked Mr Penrose[125], who paid me if your leave was not out, he sayd you have not gone twelve Months, I told him they must be the best judges of what time to apply, but you had told me long before you left England you had got leave, he said he daresay as they knew you was gone a long Voyage they would take no notice of the time,

126 Mrs Scarbrough, a family friend.
127 Mr and Mrs Thomas, naval friends. (See notes 114 and 115.)
128 Captain and Mrs. Brown, naval friends. (See note 115.)

I sayd I thought it best to be secure (I observed Young Mr Sykes, fetched a large parcel of letters in your hand Writing as soon as I went in, I asked him the date of your last letter he seemed, absent but soon after recolecting himself told me it had no date,) Mr S came to me and told me he had just sent the Clarke with your letter for fresh leave, I saw him go, and thought my self very fortunate in having gone, as if you should not succeed in your presant undertaking I hope you will always be able to keep that particularly if we have Peace, but that as yet seems a matter of doubt as all the ships are preparing and not a Sailor discharged. young Mr Sykes has behaved very kind to me each time I have gone. I never wish to see his Father again, as I consider him a compleate Bear.

Mr. Pearson called some time since to ask me to spend part of the Christmas with Mrs P I half promised, if he comes for me must go but had rather be excused as I find no pleasure in going out particularly in the Country this cold weather. I called on Mrs. Scarbrough[126] the other Day, she looks remarkably well inquired very kindley after you desired to be remembered, I Dined once with Mr Mrs Thomas[127] & Mrs Brown[128] since I came from Margate, Mrs T seems quite happy, but it is uncertain as yet weather Mr T is not to go back to Lord Clive, Captain Brown stays till Lord C, returns, so poor Mrs Brown like me must content herself with being

129 A wife whose husband was away for a considerable time.

130 The city of Madras was the administrative and commercial centre of British power in India.

131 The Neumans are not otherwise identified. Caroline Vache apparently became a particularly kind and gracious friend to Elizabeth.

132 Windsor Lodge, also known as Cumberland Lodge, was a house in Windsor Great Park a few miles south of Windsor Castle. It was the residence from 1765 to 1790 of Henry Frederick, Duke of Cumberland and Strathearn, brother of King George III. After his death in 1790 it was occupied by his widow, Anne, until 1803. William Waterhouse's business at Windsor Lodge in 1801 appears to have been related to trying to preserve favours he had previously received from Cumberland, probably in the years when he served the Duke as a page.

133 China Island, evidently also known as the Chinese Island, was an island in a landscaped lake with a Chinese-style building on it. Apparently William Waterhouse received a £20 sinecure in connection with it.

134 Henry Frederick, Duke of Cumberland and Strathearn, brother of King George III.

a Widow bewitched.[129] she hopes if you should go
to Madrass[130] you will go and see Capt B they all
desire to be remembered, as does Miss Vache Caroline
Mr & Mrs Neuman,[131] inshort all my friends. my
Old friend Mrs Ward I fear is going very fast, she
beged Lady Bensley would let me know she wished
to see me as soon as I came from Margate, I went
and spent the Day with her in Aldergate Street where
she is on a visit, she told me she intended taking a
House at Croyden, and should be very happy if I
would go and stay with her till Your return, or as
long as I liked she should be happy of my Company,
she has lost the use of one side near these twelve
Months. I went again last week poor thing I was
really shocked to see the alteration, she as ever shown
the partiality of a Mother for me, and if she could
would always have me with her, from her preseant
appearance she will never move from the House were
she is till called to a better World, in her I shall loose
a great and sincere friend.

my Father is gone for two Days to Windsor
Lodge[132], amongst the rest of his losses he is likely
to have the China Island[133] taken from him it is
very hard as that twenty pounds a Year is all he
ever had for living four and twenty Years with the
Duke of Cumberland[134], he has not been well for
some time and in my opinion looks very Ill it makes
my Heart ahce [ache] when I look at his pale Face
and hollow Cheeks, indeed he is always fretting

135 Mr Presgraves, presumably young William Waterhouse's employer.

136 Elizabeth Bass to George Bass, 15 December 1801, ZML MSS 6544, ML, Sydney.

O my God if we should loose such a Father. I always tell him he fancies he looks ill, he has had a bowel complaint Bowels [*sic*] some time, it is over and I hope he will soon look better, he stais at home a great deal too much I wish I could get him out. Henry is better than when I wrote last and gone to Portsmouth he has no Ship. William is likely to leave Spalding as Mr Presgraves[135] affairs are very bad, poor fellow Ill luck seems to follow him. the rest are all well and doing the best they can, all desire their Love and join me in Comp'ts and best wishes to Captain Bishop. this my ever dear George is the 18th Letter I have written you, I hope it will not miss as those did I wrote in January Febuary & March, it was hard you should have no Letters but shurely, you did not for a moment think I could neglect you never my Love that God almighty bless prosper and preserve you is the wish of your truely affectionate Wife Eliz'th Bass[136]

George Bass to Elizabeth Bass

Venus in Matavai Bay Otaheiti [Tahiti] Jan. 30. 1802

My beloved Bess.
I have ever written to thee when an opportunity offered; I wrote from Port Jackson before we sailed

137   Hawaiian Islands.

138   Bass' expectations of his wife's very proper conduct were typical of the time.

upon this part of the voyage. I lament much it was inconvenient, hazardous, & impossible to take thee with me upon our voyage from England, which I fear must be very very long. However my love ever consider it is now too late, by no means set out to attempt to join me at Port Jackson; no not even if thy father or thy brother Henry wl'd go there, for we shall certainly miss each other. Whilst thou art fixed I know where to find thee, but if thou ever gettest away from the place where I expect to find thee, we may perhaps wander about after each other for years unsuccessfully. Bishop will stay on this island for four or five months whilst I take the brig to the Sandwich Islands[137] & rejoin him here. It w'd have been dangerous, thou mayest be well aware, for a married man to remain exposed for months to the temptations of 5000 handsome, naked females. My fears on this head thou dost not believe. That's right. Such females [I]'d never depreciate, but they w'd infinitely exalt thee in the opinion & esteem of thy husband. His affections instead of being estranged from thee, w'd be fixed upon thee more firmly. Be confident my love that nothing but thy own conduct can ever alienate my warm, my sincere love.[138]

The females of the Royal family who with the old King & suite too often incommode us in our little cabin, have seen thy picture (little Bess); they much admire the <u>waheine</u> of <u>Brittance</u> and are

139 George Bass to Elizabeth Bass, 30 January 1802, ZML MSS 6544, ML, Sydney.

much pleased when they hear that I will bring her by & by to visit them in person.

Their acquaintance my love w'd however do thee no great honor, not after a few days w'd they afford thee much pleasure, but w'd create disgust.

The young king cannot visit us, he & his queen are carried on mens shoulders, & every place they enter is their own as well as every place or thing they touch. They are two sad wretches.

Adieu my love for a few months   G Bass[139]

Elizabeth Bass to George Bass

Tichborne Street February 5th 1802
This is the 5th letter I have sent to China

My dear George
What can I have to say, yet I cannot let any opertunity slip, as it may be very long before any other ships go out, if you get all my Scrawls I think you will be heartily tired of reading them as this will make the 23 since you left me, tho from not receiving them, my George has half accused his poor Bess of neglecting him, it is not so my Love, well I forgive you, if I had not been more fortunate perhaps I should have done the same. our House had been a very miserable one for some

140 Sir Gilbert Blane, naval physician. (See Biographical notes.) William Waterhouse's earlier service as page to the Duke of Cumberland, brother of George III, may have been instrumental in bringing Blane to Maria's bedside.

141 George Bass was baptised in the church of St Denis in Aswarby, Lincolnshire, on 3 February 1771. He was born probably on 30 January.

time past, my Sister Maria was very Ill with a
Cough and Weasing at her Stomach, I understand
she has had it upwards of these twelve Months
in a small degree, but it seemed to have taken
thorough possesion of her, I advised my Father
to ask Doctor Blane[140] to see her, he came ordered
her to be Bled and Blistered, and take a variety of
Medicines, for some time her life seemed doubtful,
but thank God she is now able to go down Stairs.
my father had been confined this Month, first with
sore throat and since with the Gout in both Knees
and Feet, at one time I was very fearful of it going
to his Stomach as he felt uncommon pains, being
a Doctors Wife and chief Nurse, I gave plenty
of Brandy, (you used to tell me to give it your
Mother) I hope it has the desired efect as he is able
to hobble down in the drawing Room tho as yet
both Feet are tied up in a Blanket. on Wednesday
last we all drank to your health, two Birth Days[141]
and O there must be a third, time goes so slow and
your fate so uncertain, but I must not think of it
or I shall write no more. my Sister Amelia has had
a bad fever and sore throat is getting very well
again. so you see your little Wife being an Idle
person has had her time imployed in Nursing the
Sick, and by no means well her self, In my last I
told you I had a very bad pain in my Left Side so
much so as to prevent my turning in Bed without
violent pain, at times it swels inwardly, and goes

142 Mr Concedent, presumably a surgeon.
143 A substance derived from the antler of a hart; a source of ammonia.
144 John Wolcot, physician and satirist best known by his pseudonym of Peter Pindar. (See Biographical notes.)
145 No explanation of this comment appears to exist.

down again, Mr Concedent[142] ordered me to rub it with Hartshorn[143] and Oil and to be cautious not to lift anything or exert myself, I did so for two Months, but it got no better and he was gone out of Town,

I drank Tea at Miss Vaches about a Fort night since I was fortunate enough to meet with Doctor Wolcot (or Peter Pindar)[144] there he congratulated me on my Mariage, talked of you in high terms, from what he had herd and hoped I was perfectly well, I told him of the pain in my side, he inquired all the particulars about it, and sayd as he had saved my Life once[145] he would be my Doctor again, and if I chose till my own [i.e. George Bass] returned he ordered me a Strengthening Plaster to cover the Side for a Month, if that did not succeed my Father was to let him know and he would give me Medicine. but like you does not wish to give it unless absolutely necessary, he abuses the Doctors and Physicians, says they are a set of Rogues and play in each others Hands, and for that reason he will have no farther to do with it than to assist a friend, that my George was so like your self, I have a high opinion of him and if I do not get rid of this unpleasant companion at the Months end shall trouble him, I fear it is detirmined to stay by me as I have worn the Plaster this fornight and it is very little better, tho it has not had a fair trial, as I went in the City to see my

146 Elizabeth's sick elderly friend in Aldergate Street.
147 Mrs Ward was evidently staying at Lady Bensley's residence.
148 Eliza Kent, née Kent, d. 1810, cousin and wife of William Kent. She accompanied him on some of his voyages. She would be sailing shortly with her husband for New South Wales. (See 'Kent, William', Biographical notes.)

poor friend Mrs Ward[146] coming home in a dark
Street I fell over a projecting step of a Door,
bruised my self very much, inshort shook my hole
fraim but thank God broke no Bones fortunately
one of Lady Bensley[147] Maids came home with me
from Mrs W or I might have lay in the Street till
some one had picked me up, as I was so stuned by
the fall I could not move, and fancied I had fell in
a Sellar, I have so far got the better of it as only
to feel my Arm stiff in change of Weather, but it
shook my side, I supose you think it is quite time
to have done with this dismal tale. well then my
dear George, the next thing to tell you is I was
very much entertained with Doctor Wolcots
conversation, and discription of many parts of his
Work, there are two publications, since the last I
sent you, I went in the City but could not get them
or I would have sent them by Mrs. Kent[148], I am
in Love with Doctor Blane, this is a pretty
declaration for a Wife, stop my George I will tell
you, the day I went for the Books he called to see
Maria, she said her Sister Bass had always mixed
her medicines, he imediately repeated Bass Bass
what Bass the Surgeon, Maria said my sisters
Husband, he gave my Mother joy, then went up
to see my Father, gave him joy and told him his
Daughter had Maried one of the finest fellows in
the world inshort spoke of you with rapture,
wished much to have seen me, you may be shure

149 From 1799 to 1805 HMS *Buffalo*, 462 tons, served the colony of New South Wales mainly under the command of Lieutenant William Kent. Its establishment was the quota of officers and men assigned to the ship. (See 'Kent, William', Biographical notes.)

all this won my warm Heart but it was his last Visit, therefore there is no danger my Love.

I go to Dine with Miss Vache reagularly once a Week she is very partial and kind to me, I missed this and she sent to know the reason they took me with them to the Opera, I was as much entertained, as I can expect to be while you are from me, all the will [while] I was there, O how I wished you to have been of the party, it was the only place I ever remember you to have had a desire to go to, and it did not open till after you was gone.

Leiutenant Kent, I believe is made Captain, the Buflow[149] is put on the same establishment as the Reliance was and has been expected to Sail for Port Jackson for sometime, Mrs Kent and her Youngest Child go out again I have called on her twice (given her the Papers a Seal and Watch paper for you, as a trifling remembrance from your poor little Wife, will my George wear it for my sake, O how I wish I could tell what you want from England how happy I should be to send it but that cannot be, when shall I have another Letter from you, that is the only comfort I can now receive but they tell me the soonest I can expect to hear will be next March, well I must be contented, but if ever we meet again my Love it must be to part no more, it is cruel it is indeed my George, you must take me with you, I can bear Sea Sickness and hardship better than a seperation from you,

150   Mrs Stewart, the Waterhouses' friend in Margate.
151   Mr and Mrs Norvill, friends of the Waterhouse family.
152   James Price was listed on *Venus'* crew list as an 'apprentice' and evidently served as Bass' servant. Apparently his mother was in the employ of the Norvills and in her letters to Bass, Elizabeth occasionally passed messages from mother to son.

I often think I ought to have gone. I fear you would meet with bad success at Port Jackson, as I had a Letter from Mrs. Stewart[150] last Week she tells me, her son John who is in India, wrote her word he was in Port Jackson in August and that they sold their goods for three Hundred per Cent, I fear they would get there just before you and stock the Market, pray dont let all these disapointments hurt your Health and Spirits all your friends know, you will do your best, and if you do not succeed as well as you could wish this Voyage you may the next, you are Young and if all fails, you have still a genteel profession. my Father and me called at Mr Sykes just before he was confined, I asked Mr S if your leave was renewed he told me they had forgot to send, but there was not a doubt of it and if there should they would see to it, Young Mr S is always very kind, we went from there and spent the Day at Mr. Norvils,[151] they beged to be kindly remembered, your Servants Mother[152] came to thank me for having remembered her in my Letters I promised to ask you to tell him she was well and will be much obliged if you will let me know how he is and goes on that I may let her know. she has had one Letter from him he says he is very happy and speaks highly of you. my Brother Henry is still at Admiral Phillips, we expect him in London every Day, as the Lawyers expect his trial for the Prize money to come on

153 William Waterhouse, brother of Elizabeth Bass.
154 Young William's 'fashionable complaint' appears to have been a popular malady known as 'spleen', characterised by depression, 'odd and irregular ideas' and 'vapours'. Also called 'the English malady', references to it appear in serious dissertations and in literature.
155 See note 129.
156 Elizabeth's meaning here is not clear.
157 George Johnston, army officer and New South Wales landholder. (See note 99.)

very soon, poor fellow I hope he will get it, I am
shure he deserves it, and in my opinion is very Ill
used as it [we?] certainly think it is his right we
had a Letter from William[153] to Day he is still at
Spalding, has the Fashionable complaint[154] this has
been the most sickly Winter that has been known,
in all parts of England, and a colder one, I always
allow myself a fire in my little Room to write by.
but O my dear dear George how I miss you these
cold Nights, if it was the last Winter I was to spend
a poor Widow bewitched[155] I could bear it better,
but there is yet another to pass before I shall be
blessed with a dear Husband, how do you bear the
cold country you are now in, do you often think of
your little Wife, yes my dear George I know you
do. pray give my best Comp'ts to Captain Bishop
tell him I never sing now, but on your return I
shall not forget for Batchelors what great news[156]
I long to help you plague [tease] him as I used to
do, pray has he the Gout yet, or does his attention
to little Venus keep it off, I suppose on his return
your Mother and he will settle the buisness [their
relationship?], I wrote to her Yesterday and asked
her if she thought as much of her Bishop as I do
of my George. the last letter I had from her she
was as well as the Gout will let her be.

Major Jonstone[157] called at the begining of last
Week was just come up from Portsmouth, had
been down to get every thing ready on board the

158 John Hunter, governor of New South Wales 1795–1800. (See Biographical notes.)

159 Evidently David Collins, officer of the Marines and first lieutenant-governor of Tasmania. He arrived in Australia with the First Fleet and served as judge-advocate and secretary to Governor Phillip. He established a settlement at Port Phillip, which was soon moved to the present site of Hobart. He wrote *An Account of the English Colony in New South Wales* in two volumes.

160 Anthony Fenn Kemp arrived in New South Wales as an officer of the New South Wales Corps. He pioneered notably as a merchant and grazier in Tasmania.

161 The son Elizabeth met was probably John Jamison, then about 26 years old and a naval surgeon. While on Norfolk Island, however, Thomas Jamison had had two illegitimate sons by a convict, Elizabeth Colley.

Buflow for his Voyage and intended going for good on Sunday last but promised to call the last thing for another Letter, he has not done so and as he has alway been very attentive I fear he is Ill, had my Father been able he would have called on him, Gover H[158] Colonel Collings[159] and Major Jonstone went to Portsmouth to gether, they had got within a few Miles when the Coach over set in a ditch M-J at the bottom the rest all on him, his Head was much bruised and mashed just above the Temple and he thinks there is Glas [glass] remaining in his Head the Governor hurt his lame shoulder, and Colonel Collings much bruised. what will be the end of Major Jonstones Voyage I know not but every step he takes towards it seems unfortunate. the Buflow will be well stoed [stowed] with Port J [paper torn] People, Captain Mrs Kent and Child Major [paper torn] Captain Kemp[160], and Mr Jamisons Son as [paper torn] I have seen him but twice he seems a pleasant young Man much of the Gentleman, we were astonished when Major Jonstone introduced him as we thought the Daughter he brought to [paper torn] House was the Eldest, but I supose they must have been Maried before he went to Port Jackson still it is strange we never shoud have heard of Mr Jamisons having such a Son[161], there seems to be strange tricks in that place called [word obscured] Jackson, pray always remember my dear George you have

162 This letter appears to be lost.
163 Elizabeth Bass to George Bass, 5 February 1802, ZML MSS
6544, ML, Sydney.

a Wife in England and [word obscured] for you alone Mr Williamson was to go out as Deputy Comessary but weather he is able or not I cannot tell, the last time I herd of him he was very Ill, but since the affair at Mr Norvils he is never spoken of, he made a very valuable Servant in the family [word scratched out] the little time he was there, but I gave you the particulars in my last.[162] all my Family desire their Love, my Father talks as much of you as if you had been his own Son and I am shure is as fond of you, is always very kind to me. Comp'ts from all friend. God almighty bless preserve and send you safe home to me my ever dear George

>Your truely affectionate Wife
>Eliz'th Bass[163]

Elizabeth's reference to matters about which she says she had previously written to George again confirms the loss of letters on their uncertain journey across the oceans.

Lost letters have made something of a mystery of an incident that at about this time involved Elizabeth and George's long-time friend Matthew Flinders. In February 1800, several months after Bass' departure from Port Jackson for England, Flinders wrote Bass a letter, which, on sailing himself for England, he probably left in Sydney for Bass to pick up on his return to the colony. Flinders wrote of commercial possibilities the two men had discussed and the publication of their charts and a book George had

164 Elizabeth Bass, note on letter from Matthew Flinders to George
Bass, 15–21 February 1800, ZML MSS 7046, ML, Sydney.

considered writing. Flinders then went on to mention the various friendships he had enjoyed, and the hero-worship he had felt for Bass when he was younger. Seemingly the letter was forwarded to England, where, since Bass may have sailed with the *Venus*, it appears to have been given to Elizabeth. Elizabeth's reaction was astonishingly hostile. On the address wrapper she wrote:

> this George is written by a Man that bears a bad Character no one has seen this letter but I could tell you many things that makes me dislike him rest ashured he is no friend of yours or any ones farther than his own interest is concerned. Elizth Bass[164]

Whether or not she had read the letter is not known, and there is only speculation as to why Elizabeth felt such antipathy for Flinders, whom she had previously described as being kind and helpful. Any letter she may have written in explanation is evidently among those that disappeared. Another unknown is whether Bass received Flinders' letter. What is obvious, however, is that the two friends continued writing to each other as before.

On 6 February 1802 George Bass and the *Venus* sailed from Tahiti, steering north across some 3000 miles of almost empty ocean to reach Hawaii on 11 March. Here for five months he navigated through a mainly uncharted archipelago of volcanic mountain tops rising from the depths of the ocean, exchanging European manufactures for hogs, salt and fresh provisions. The means by which

THE LETTERS OF GEORGE & ELIZABETH BASS

George Bass sent letters from Hawaii to Elizabeth and to his mother is not clear. However, since their European discovery by James Cook in 1778, the islands had been visited sporadically by American and European ships, and by the early 1800s the American whaling fleet had begun to winter there. Somewhere off the island of Molokai Bass encountered someone prepared to set several letters on their way to England.

George Bass to Elizabeth Bass

Venus off Morokoi, Sandwich Islands [Molokai,
Hawaii] May 20. 1802

I write to thee my beloved Bess at all opportunities and what have I to say or what have I ever said but assurances of love and unshaken attachment. I could tell thee of all my proceedings in this protracted, untoward & most laborious voyage; but to what purpose. All that I say to thy father and brother is said also to thee. Eighteen months Bess thou gavest me for my voyage; alas, alas. I often wish thee with me. My Bess w'd be delighted with this place, or with that say I to myself; but again it sometimes happens. oh how much the presence of my beloved wife would aggravate this temporary distress I feel. In short bad as it is, it is best that thou art not with me. Be asured that meet

165 George Bass to Elizabeth Bass, 20 May 1802, ZML MSS 6544, ML, Sydney.

we will when we possibly can. It is far for thee to
come to me, it is nothing for me to sail thousands
of miles to pick thee up & carry thee away. A smile
of fortune may do much as a frown has already
done. Sh'd I ever establish a commerce in New
South Wales. I will fetch thee if I build a small
vessel for the purpose. At present I have no
thoughts of the kind altho' some feeble perceptions
of the possibility of such a change with the warming
glimpse of sunshine that the living with thee once
more w'd occasion. Being now amongst the Islands
trading with canoes & taking care of the vessel
takes up every instant of the day, and often night.
I can only find time to assure thee once again of
firm unalterable love for my beloved Wife
    Adieu Geo Bass[165]

In this short, intimate letter Bass suggested more of his
activities, his hopes and his emotions than usual. The
beauty of the Hawaiian islands slips obliquely through. A
sapphire sea sparkling under a dazzling sun, white-edged
beaches and slender waterfalls flowing down steep green
mountainsides—these, he knows, would have delighted his
Bess. There is the warmth of his desire to live with her,
the creeping hope of a ship and a business in New South
Wales to sustain them, as he steers cautiously among the
islands in unfamiliar waters. There is, too, a glimpse of the
labour involved, with island chiefs on board at all hours
for long negotiations, outrigger canoes loaded with hogs

166   George Bass to Thomas Jamison, 15 May 1802, in Michael Roe, 'New Light on George Bass, Entrepreneur and Intellectual', *Journal of the Royal Australian Historical Society*, vol. 72, Part 5, 1987, p. 264.

167   George Bass to Sarah Bass, 20 May 1802, ZML MSS 6544, ML, Sydney.

168   Philip Gidley King to Lord Hobart, 15 November 1802, *HRA*, vol. III, ed. Frederick Watson, 1915, p. 724.

coming alongside the *Venus*, the raising of shrieking pigs to the deck, sometimes by lantern light. 'The labour,' he would write to his friend Thomas Jamison, 'is no mean trifle.'[166] From Molokai Bass wrote also to his 'dearest friend', his mother. He would, he said, visit all the islands a second time 'by way of gleaning the field', before sailing south for Tahiti and Bishop's pork-curing operation.

Bass reached Matavai Bay on 1 August 1802. He had written to his mother that he would then 'jog down together [with Bishop] through the Friendly [Samoa], Society, Navigators [Tonga], Feejees & Hebrides [Vanuatu] on our way to Port Jackson'.[167] To explore the island-strewn ocean further was clearly an irresistible opportunity for Bass, and he evidently made all these stops with the exception of the Fiji Islands.

On 15 November 1802 Governor King wrote to the Secretary of State for War and the Colonies, Robert Hobart, Baron Hobart and Earl of Buckinghamshire: 'Mr. Bass arrived here with the Venus the 14th inst., from Otaheite with 57 tons of salted pork.'[168]

George Bass to Elizabeth Bass

Venus Port Jackson Nov'r 15. 1802

Two minutes must suffice to tell thee I love thee; and that I am yet alive as thou mayest perhaps surmise by my writing to thee. The Naturaliste bound to

169   In the harbour were anchored HMS *Buffalo*, Lieutenant William Kent, the French scientific exploration vessels, *Naturaliste* and *Géographe*, and the convict transports *Alexander* and *Atlas*.

France sails in a few hours; we are just arrived, with a complete cargo of Pork b[r]ought back.

The speculation has answered, but its weight as a counterbalance to our bad success is trifling. Perseverance, industry, economy and a few other biting qualities will I trust yet clear our luck. Time ah time my beloved must produce this change and our long hard, but I trust last as well as first separation must be lengthened by it. Be good, be estimable and though this same Time may wrinkle your lean <u>kissing</u> chops I shall only consider it as answerable to the improvements he will also have made on my anxious brow.

Mrs. Kent desires her kind Compts. I have just left the Buffaloe where I dined.[169] Wait my beloved—but I shall only talk of impossibilities and so tell your dear father & brother the next conveyance they will hear from me as usual.

Bishops ill health has thrown all cares & concerns upon my hands both for ship & cargo and for some time they must remain those. But anxiety of mind has long been my most familiar acquaintance; bad company you will say my dear; but so it is!

Adversity is a good grindstone for the wits perhaps; but its very rough in its operations, I must needs say. I am however now getting smoothened down with a drenching of P. Pindars <u>Oil of fool</u> administered by the hand of Mr. Baudin the French

170   Nicolas Thomas Baudin, *c.* 1750–1803, French navigator and
      explorer in command of the French scientific expedition that left
      Le Havre on 19 October 1800 to chart the Australian coasts.
      In 1802 the French ships spent several months in Sydney.
171   Bass had accompanied Governor Philip Gidley King and
      Lieutenant William Kent on board the French *Naturaliste*.
      Preceded by his reputation of having discovered Bass Strait
      and his attempt to cross the Blue Mountains, he was lavishly
      complimented by the French officers. Always realistic about
      his own achievements, Bass accepted the praise in the spirit of
      Pindar's satirical verse. Paul Brunton, Senior Curator, Mitchell
      Library, Sydney, suggests that *Oil of Fool* may have been one of
      Wolcot's books. (See 'Wolcot, John', Biographical notes.)
172   George Bass to Elizabeth Bass, 15 November 1802, ZML MSS
      6544, ML, Sydney.

Commodore[170] who is collecting curiosities for the National Museum & has threatened me with a niche in the Glass case. So much for that;—it will please thee perhaps nor can I be angry at it; but thou shalt go into the Glass case too.[171] I wrote to thee from Otaheiti in Feb. & from the Sandwich Isles in May last.

God of the World spare thee and make thee happy & keep thee. Now thats a fine prayer you'll say. I am no Parson Bess but I promised the Parson I would love thee truly & so I ever will as long as thou deservest it. Adieu   G Bass[172]

George Bass to Elizabeth Bass

Venus Port Jackson 21 December 1802

My beloved Bess

In order that I may not break through my constant rule of writing to thee by every conveyance I send thee this but a ship by China will sail in a few days and I shall then write to thee more fully.

We are preparing for another voyage to the S. Sea Islands for pork, but it is not that alone which is the object of our voyage. If performed, I propose to turn homeward where I hope to see thee well and ready to take a trip with me to this side of the globe for I will never again quit England without thee. I shall write by the next ship to thy

173 George Bass to Elizabeth Bass, 21 December 1802, ZML MSS 6544, ML, Sydney.

174 George Bass to Henry Waterhouse, 1 January 1803, ZML MSS 6544, ML, Sydney.

175 South American members of the camel family. The guanaco (*Lama guanacoe*) ranges wild from the snowline to sea level through the length of the Andes Mountains. The alpaca (*Lama pacos*) is a domesticated animal kept and bred for its wool.

father and brothers with sincere love & complements
to them all believe me thy affectionate
Geo Bass[173]

Here there was for Elizabeth an intimation that before
heading for England Bass had other plans in mind. On
1 January 1803 he went further in a letter to Henry
Waterhouse, remarking that his second pork-hunting
voyage was about to commence, but that the voyage was not
'altogether for pork. I mean to cross the South Pacific upon
a venture... If this voyage ends anything near what I expect
I shall then turn my head homeward as a Sealer.'[174]

Four days later he wrote to his father-in-law further
detailing his plans for the voyage: a stop at New Zealand's
Dusky Bay where the wreck of an old East Indiaman, the
Endeavour, could yield useful pieces of iron and timber,
and an arrangement with Governor King for the purchase,
if it was repairable, of the colonial brig *Norfolk*, which
almost a year before had been wrecked on the beach at
Tahiti's Matavai Bay.

Trade with the Spanish colonies of Peru and Chile had
been very much on Bass' mind for several years. While
the sale of foreign goods to South American buyers was
forbidden, the Spanish colonial government allowed certain
purchases to be made by the English. Bass' proposal was to
buy cattle or, alternatively, native guanacos and alpacas[175],
animals he believed would serve well in New South Wales.
For this entirely legitimate trade Bass had received from
Governor King a certificate attesting to his purpose being

176 George Bass to William Waterhouse, 5 January 1803, *HRNSW,* vol. V, ed. F.M. Bladen, William Applegate Gullick, Government Printer, Sydney, 1896, pp. 1–3.

to procure food supplies and livestock for breeding in New South Wales. But Bass' thinking went beyond this. His letter of 5 January 1803 to William Waterhouse contains an extraordinary paragraph in Spanish that translates:

> During the time that I shall be in the ports of New Spain I shall not be idle with regard to secret commerce for which I go prepared and [promptly] ready.[176]

With little doubt, if the opportunity presented, Bass intended to engage in contraband trade, probably to dispose of some of his unsold English merchandise. His use of Spanish in writing to William Waterhouse remains unexplained. It is, however, obvious that George Bass' plans for his second voyage into the Pacific involved much more than simply the purchase of pigs and the salting of pork.

On 3 January he wrote to Elizabeth at greater length than usual, a fond, teasing, punning missive that contained no reference to his up-coming voyage.

George Bass to Elizabeth Bass

Venus Sydney Cove Jan 3 1803

My beloved Bess

I have already written to thee twice since my arrival here from the Islands and shall now write again.

177 Letters were typically closed by a person's seal impressed on melted wax. Elizabeth had either used her own seal's impression on a letter or possibly sent George the seal itself.

178 Watchpapers, generally intended as sentimental mementos, were disks of paper, silk or other materials inscribed or painted with a decorative device and made to fit into the back of a pocket watch case. The watchpaper sent by Elizabeth was evidently decorated in some way to represent her.

179 Bass, on sick leave from the navy, was on half-pay, less than five shillings a day (Keith M. Bowden, *George Bass 1771–1803, His Discoveries, Romantic Life and Tragic Disappearance*, Oxford University Press, Melbourne, 1952, p. 95), half of which was remitted to Elizabeth, the other half to his mother.

I cannot therefore have much more to tell thee than that I love thee [words indecipherable] that I am writing large to make my story look a long one; that I rec'd thy Seal[177] and that I hope ever to have reason to esteem it for thy sake; the watchpaper[178] is I suppose a representation of thee; that little Bess is well and still presides over the Timekeeper staring me in the face with her large eyes and reminding me of thee every morning as I am winding up that machine.—that I desire my kind love to thy sisters for whom if they are not married 'ere this I will, tell them, drop a tear when I get into the habit of crying.

(Dear Wife, do my love get into the habit of spelling a little better; thou art a most notorious destroyer of good old english. I have mended my pen to give thee the above advice that thou might see it more Pointedly.

Bess when I return if thou misspellest one word out of three only, great as the amendment will be, I will not stand to a chair to be kissed and thou knowest well that thy short legs will never reach me from the ground. So take care.

I could tell thee much about poverty & the [word indecipherable] but that is needless since thou must be in the way of feeling it by the makeup of the sum I remit to thee.[179]

God bless thee my love now I am really grown sad again but I wish a few happy years are yet in

180   An income that is sufficient to live on.

181   A reference to Elizabeth's mention of her friend Mrs Brown, wife of the absent Captain Brown, and evidently also herself.

store for us. With my wife I could labour more cheerfuly, for labour must long be my lot. All I wish for is to be able to give thee comfortable accomodation in a cabin large enough to take exercise and then we will sail all over the world together in search of a competence.[180]

Our Bro'r William I have never written to since I left England. I have done wrong and must shortly mend my error. I much esteem his character. The two poor bewitched widows[181] you say are well. Pray present to them my wishes for their relief & their happiness.

I wish Bess I could just put out my arm across the globe and grapple thee. I'll warrant I'd bring thee over. But I am called off; it is my dear to visit a lady, a lady too of much fashion & beauty, one whom I much esteem for love her I dare not, as you know. Well, then my dear not to teeze you any longer. I am called in the way of my profession.— The lady has a scabby bottom, which I mean to inspect most minutely for such a sight you know my dear is seldom to be seen.

Well, I have seen her bottom and have recommended the use of copper to be applied in large sheets. But if I may be allowed to speak to you of the make shape & various beauties of that bottom I must at once tell you Venus herself shows not one more delicate.

182 Perhaps a teasing reference to the women of the Pacific islands, seemingly in response to a letter in the same spirit from Elizabeth, now lost.

183 George Bass to Elizabeth Bass, 3 January 1803, ZML MSS 6544, ML, Sydney.

184 A fishwife, with a reference to Elizabeth's sometimes sharp tongue.

185 George Bass to William Waterhouse, 2 February 1803, *HRNSW*, vol. V, ed. F.M. Bladen, Sydney, 1896, p. 15.

By the bye I thank you much for the saving commission you have sent me amongst the ladies black blue & yellow. I'm sorry my love I cant return you the compliment[182]

There's no end to writing to you, yes You and so no more from your loving husband <u>till death us do part</u>. Do you remember that Bess

Geo Bass[183]

On 2 February 1803, three days before his final sailing from New South Wales, Bass wrote to his father-in-law, again referring to his plans for the voyage. Of the proposed fishery at the southern end of New Zealand, he wrote: 'The fishery is not to be set in motion till after my return to old England, when I mean to seize upon my dear Bess, bring her out here, and make a *poissarde*[184] of her, where she cannot fail to find plenty of use for her tongue.'[185]

There was no reference to other commercial activities aside from the pork trade. However, two earlier letters are mentioned, which evidently never reached England.

Probably in mid-January Bass travelled to the inland settlement of Parramatta to farewell friends residing there. Seemingly it was a visit that brought to the fore the burden of all that he was trying to accomplish, focusing on Elizabeth and his desperate yearning for her together with his anxieties regarding her and their future. Childbirth at this time was fraught with danger for both mother and child, and clearly Bass could not face the thought of such

186 A fishwife.
187 Fleet Market, a public market built on a covered section of
     Fleet Ditch in Holborn (1737).

an event at sea. Aboard the *Venus* in an inebriated state he wrote a pained and muddled letter.

George Bass to Elizabeth Bass

Well my Bess; — and so your father tells you you must be a fish-fag.[186] Ah, little didst thou think that when thy heart has fearfully fluttered at a glance from the fiery eye of one of those nymphs of Fleet Market[187] on thy nocturnal prowl for next days food; little didst thou imagine that 'ere long fate had decreed thee to join that land of long tongued corps.

I am just come down from Parramatta where I have been taking leave of Mrs Kent Mrs—— & Mrs. many more previous to going to sea. In all my walks, at every beautiful prospect in every pleasantly situated house—but hold Bess I am going to give thee proofs I love thee when I ought to give thee only words. In short Bess they all bring thee into my mind. Thou shalt one day or other admire them with me—that is if thou art a good—old woman.—for if thou art bad thou mayest 'een stay in England, we have enough of that sort here. Again.

Thou shalt not breed. & fill my cabin full of squallers, there's no room for such gentry. No the sea air will make thee fat as a hog. Delicate comparison, say you Why my Bess dont get upon

188 'Darby and Joan' first appeared in a poem in the *Gentleman's Magazine* in 1735 and came to epitomise a devoted couple who have long lived together in harmony. Bass seems to be referring to the three letters he had written to Elizabeth since his arrival in Port Jackson in November. The fourth, undated, was probably the one he was now writing. The postscript is written in a very shaky hand.

189 George Bass to Elizabeth Bass, no date [Jan? 1803] ZML MSS 6544, ML, Sydney.

that chair. I won't stand to it. Nor be climbed like a tree. Nor... Nor will I cease to love thee as thou deservest of thy Affectionate fool
    Geo Bass

Now Bess tell me what doest thou understand by all this letter, & me not drunk.
    3rd epistle, Darby to Joan[188] within 2 months. 3rd. 4th by Jan [or June][189]

Reading this letter, undated, confused and unkind, with a scrawled, almost illegible postscript—so 'unlike your Self', as she later wrote—brought to the surface all Elizabeth's worry and disappointment, which she spilled into a reply of heartbreak and reproach. She read and reread Bass' letter, failing to understand it, and unfortunately it appears to have been the last she would receive from him. No letter to Elizabeth of what would seem to be a later date appears to exist. Three days before sailing, however, as previously mentioned, Bass wrote to his father-in-law, a letter which William Waterhouse would have shared with his daughter. He wrote optimistically and with typical enthusiasm of 'pleasing prospects' and 'great plans' and, somewhat enigmatically, but perhaps metaphorically, of 'digging gold in So. America'. On his return to England, he would seize his dear Bess and bring her 'out here'. That would have been a happier final word from her husband, even if it came to her indirectly. If he also wrote to his wife at this time, the letter has not survived.

190   Mrs King was in error regarding the date of Bass' sailing. Governor King's official list of ships clearing 'Outwards in the harbour of Port Jackson' gives the date of the departure of Bass and the *Venus* as 5 February.

Some months later Elizabeth received a letter from Anna Josepha King, Governor King's wife, who had been among those from whom Bass took final leave.

Anna Josepha King to Elizabeth Bass

New South Wales—May the 16th 1803

My dear Mrs Bass—
On the 7th[190] of last Feb'y your better half Sailed for Otaheiti, in <u>perfect good health and Spirits</u> I promised my self that I would by the first opportunity inform you of it—which pleased him and let me assure you that the only wish he had—was that you had come to N-S-Wales with him—You Would not only have made your Husband Happy—but many other friends—and none more so than your humble Servant, and her <u>better half</u>—who Joins me in every good wish and congratulation on your marriage

Mr Bass tells me that it was his own fault that you did not come out with him—I request that you will, in the kindest manner—present our good wishes to all Your Family and Friends—I have the pleasure to inform you of all our Health—excepting now, and then. when poor King has a fit of gout—which confines him Six weeks and then he recovers.

191 Anna Josepha King to Elizabeth Bass, 16 May 1803, AZML MSS 6544, ML, Sydney.

I shall be very happy to hear from you, when
any opportunity offers and to be informed of
your Health will at all times give the greatest
pleasure
To
Dear Mrs. Bass
Yours affectionately
AJKing[191]

Elizabeth would have known then that, at least upon
sailing, George had been well and happy. His departure,
however, had been many months earlier, and in the interval
no letters from her husband had reached Elizabeth. For
her a great silence was descending upon the Pacific. But
Elizabeth kept writing, increasingly assailed by all the
doubts and hurt of a young wife separated so soon and
so long from her husband. In early October she faced the
third anniversary of their wedding, and again sat alone in
her room, writing a letter that reflects near panic.

Elizabeth Bass to George Bass

19 Tichborne Street October the 8th 1803

My ever Dear George
Little did I think this time three Years [ago] we
should have been so long and cruely seperated,
indeed my Love it is a very hard task to be obliged

192 Three ships sailed for England from Port Jackson on 18 May 1803, three and a half months after Bass had departed for the Pacific: HMS *Glatton*, a former East Indiaman, unusually employed in 1802 to carry convicts to New South Wales; the *Greenwich*, privately owned, and the *Venus* whaler, privately owned.

193 Mr Norvill was a friend of Charles Bishop.

194 Charles Bishop's letter may reflect that he was not, as he wrote, 'in perfect health'. Bass sailed on 5 February and would have steered east or southeast, not 'for the West ward'. Elizabeth recognised that Bishop was not a source of accurate information. (See Biographical notes.)

195 John Hunter, governor of New South Wales 1795–1800. (See Biographical notes.)

to write again, I have been expecting you every Day these Six Months past to discribe my feelings for the last Month is impossible, three ships arrived from Port Jackson, the Glatton Greenwitch & Venus, all our friends received Letters, but none for me my poor Father went to the Owners, to Deptford [naval shipyard] & inshort to every one that was likely to give him any information[192], I went to Mr Norvils[193] he showed me two Letters he had rec'd from Captain Bishop, they mention your having left P J [Port Jackson] on the 7th of February for the West ward[194], his being left at Sick quarters tho now in perfect Health, on your return you perhaps might make up your Accounts and return to Old England you might be out, 6, 7, 10, 12, 14, or 15 Months only consider one moment my George what I felt. the perhaps! and the number of Months there was a possibility it might be, before you returned to Port Jackson, my Constitution [is] good, but not strong now very much weakened by constant anxiety of Mind.

I still believe I should have Letters as I never would think you could neglect me, it seemed unlike your self. Governor Hunter[195] came and told me the Glatton gave Government dispatches to the Huzar at Sea, suposing she would be in first. I made my self certain I should have Letters, and for the moment droped the Idea of the 15 Months and fully depended on yours, to tell me the time

196 Evidently the future Sir John Jamison, son of the surgeon Thomas Jamison. John Jamison was also a naval surgeon, becoming a Physician of the Fleet before settling in New South Wales. He owned considerable land, promoted agriculture and horticulture, and took part in colonial administration. He would have been about 27 when he brought Elizabeth what was probably Bass' last letter to reach her.

you hoped to be home. I knew Captn Bishop to be a very good natured Man but had very little opinion of his understanding, hoped he might have wrote in his usual careless manner, and depended on yours to satisfy my Anctious Mind. on Thursday last Mr Jammison Jun'r[196] Brought me yours and thank God told me you left them in perfect health and Spirits. I asked how long he supposed it would be before I might hope to see you in England he suposed in 6 Months Oh my George what a length of time it seemed. still I hoped yours would confirm it, as soon as I opened it, it was without a date, and not the smallest hint of the time you hope to return only that you would come some time or other and take me out, that was if I deserved it, had you, or have you ever had reason to doubt it, all your Letters say so George, I feel it a sting I do not deserve. to see your hand Writing once more gave me more pleasure than I can discribe, and in every line remind me you had not forgotten me. yet my dear George it could not give me real satisfaction, it was written in the stile I would talk to my Child to amuse it if I had one. it is too trifling my George, I well know in every way your trials and sufferings has been great since we parted. but I chiefly know them by strangers. you have only acknowledged the receipt of one of my Letters & I know you have received many, I have sent Eight and Twenty some things in them shurely was worth

197   Elizabeth Bass to George Bass, 8 Oct 1803 [draft], ZML MSS
      6544, ML, Sydney.

taking notice of, pray my Love think me worth
your confidence, and if you cannot return when
you have half an Hour to spare, write like yourself
to me. depend on my Honour, I have never ceased
one moment to Love you or are you ever out of
my Thoughts. you tell me it is dangerious for a
Married Man to live at Otaheite, is it not more so
at Port Jackson, pray do not be persuaded to stay
there till you have been home, I am ready to go
where ever you please to take me and have no doubt
you would be happy to have me with you, altho
we have been Married three Years to Day[197]

Here Elizabeth stopped writing, clearly too despairing to
continue. It was a letter she did not finish and did not send.

Eleven days later, however, she had recovered her
control. She rewrote the letter, with the same expressions
of love and devotion, but confronting him with her fears.
It was a letter of dignity and courage with a few brave
attempts at humour.

Elizabeth Bass to George Bass

29 Tichborne Street October 19th 1803

My ever Dear George
Little did I think this time three Years [ago] we
should have been so long and cruely seperated,

198 John Hunter, governor of New South Wales 1795–1800. (See Biographical notes.)

indeed my Love it is a very hard task to write again, I have been expecting you every Day these Six Months past, to discribe my feelings the last Month is impossible, three Ships arrived from Port Jackson, the Glatton Greenwich and Venus, all our friends recd Letters but none for me, my poor Father went to the Owners to Deptford & inshort to every one that was likely to give him any information I went to Mr Norvils he showed me two Letters he had recd from Captain Bishop they mentioned your having left P J on the 7th of February for the West ward, his being left at Sick quarters tho now in perfect Health, on your return perhaps you might settle your affairs and return to Old England, you might be out 6, 7, 10, 12, 14, or 15 Months, only Guess my George one moment what I felt, the perhaps and the number of Months it might be, before you returned to Port Jackson, my constitution [is] good but not strong now very much weakened by anxiety of Mind. I still believe I should have Letters, I never would think you could neglect me, it seemed unlike your Self. Captn Hunter[198] came and told me the Glatton gave Government Dispatches to the Huzar at Sea suposing she would be in first. at last they are arrived Mr Jemmison brought me yours and a very kind one from Mrs King, thank God they tell me you are in perfect Health and good Spirits and in all your walks remember your poor Bess, how

199   In his letter of 3 October 1801 Bass acknowledged receipt of
      Elizabeth's letter of 21 February 1801.

much happier should we be together and how long
it will be, before we meet, my Dear George you
have not given me the most distant Idea, - surely
it will not be long first, my Father thinks you
are now on your passage home but I fear from
the different reports you are not returned to Port
Jackson. You tell me I am to become a Fish fag any
thing you please could I see you once more, I am
ready to go all the World over with you, do not
let them persuade you to stay any longer, surely
by this time you have made enough to satisfy the
parties concerned, and you are more to me than
all the Riches in the world, inshort my George I
cannot be happy without you. you wish me to tell
you what I understand by your Letter, indeed I
cannot you must come and explain it, I only wish
it had been longer I well know how much fatiegue
and anxiety of Mind you must have why not tell
me all, you wish me to tell you all my cares I do so
and would gladly share yours, I have written you
Eight & Twenty Letters, but you do not mention
having recd any of them[199], shurely some things
in them where worth answering, if you do not I
declare I will not get on the Chair you may hold
your proud Head as high as you please I will not
Climbe, or fill your Cabin with Squallers, you
say you will Love me if I deserve it, had you or
have you any reason to doubt it, my Love I feel
it a Sting I do not deserve, Mrs King tells me the

200   A reference to the letter in which George urged her to expand
      her knowledge in order to be able 'to instruct me upon my
      return from my wild uncivilised voyage'.
201   Elizabeth had obviously learned of Thomas Jamison's sons by
      Elizabeth Colley. (See note 161.)

only wish you had, was that I had gone out with you Oh I wish I had, but it is now too late to think of it I would gladly take my passage out in these Ships but the fear of missing you.

I had a kind Letter from Mr Inness last Week informing me he had herd from you and that you was going to reside another Twelve Months amongst the Savages, that I hope is not the case or how shall I civilize you[200], you told me it was dangerious for a Married Man to stay there and that I should not believe your fears on their account. but have I no fears for the more Civilized Females of Port Jackson, it is a bad School for a Young, & Married Man, the Elder Mr Jammison has set his son no good example[201], I hope his friend [George Bass] has not followed it, I will have no Young one George if there are any remember they ought to be at least five Years of Age.

Mr & Mrs Bennet where in London some Months since, he is still on Shore. we have nothing but Soldiers parading the Streets it is common to see a Thousand to gether, there is great talk of an Invasion, how it will end God only knows all our Males in London are Volenteers the Taxes are more than doubled, orders are sent to all the Inhabitents of the Sea Ports to leave at an Hours notice to make room for the troops Oh my dear George if you are coming home I hope you will escape the French I had a letter from your Mother

202   Lieutenant Ingles is not otherwise identified.

last Week she is tolerably well, but very uneasy at your stay, and not having recd two Letter you mention having written her from Port Jackson with <u>Endorses</u> [endorsements?] and large remitances to Mr Sykes beged I would go there and inquire for them my Father went, Mr S fully expected them and told the Creditors he should be enabled to pay them, in consiquence of which they have all been to him, but he had received no such thing, or has my Father ever had the two Letters you mention. Lieutanant Ingles[202] told me two or three Ships Sailed from Port Jackson for the East Indies, between the French Ship and the Glatton at that time you must have been there, as we have not herd of their arrival Hope we may yet receive them.

I shall write to your Mother to Day, I am shure my George it will give you pleasure to hear we are in the most friendly terms, she tells me all her cares & all the little pleasures, they are but few we are both too fond of you to be happy in your absence indeed Sir you must behave very well to me or you will be scratched out of her Books, as I believe she knows not which of us she likes the best, I much wish to see her, and would go as you are not to be expected, but it is too expensive I fully expected you would have sent your Affidavit we have only recd one twelve Months, on account of your having omited signing one, Mr Sykes wished

203 James Price was apparently Bass' servant on board the *Venus*. (See note 152.)

me to have done it, but I declined it, I have no
particular inclination to Swing, or be transported,
unless I could be certain by it I should meet you,
in that case I realy think I should be tempted
to steal something. young Prices[203] Mother is
determined to go out with me as Servant if we
have your leave, poor woman she is much hurt at
her Sons not having written her, why did you not
make him do so, I requested you would but I fear
you have not recd half my Letters God Almighty
bless and preserve you my Love Your ever True
and Affectionate Wife Elizth Bass

P S my Brothr Henry has no Ship yet, resides in the
Country, he finds his Health much better there, is
very much disappointed at having no Letters from
you or Governor King, I think they must have been
detained, for I cannot supose you would neglect
him, he is very kind to me and has your interest
throughly at heart inshort there are very few [word
indecipherable] so good and Affectionate a[s] he
art, poor fellow he is too generious to all his Family
for his income. my Brother William still resides
in Lincoln Shire, is now very unwell owing to a
kick in the back by his Horse this time Twelve
Months, congealed Blood had lodged in his inside
ever since, he has lately brought up a large lump,
and there still remains more, I fear poor fellow it
is a serious thing. Doctor Blane called last Week

204   Andrew Douglas White, born in 1793, was the son of John White, Surgeon General to the New South Wales colony, and Rachel Turner, a convict. The boy was sent to England to join his father in 1800, but evidently was left largely in the care of the Waterhouse family. Andrew eventually joined the Royal Engineers and fought bravely at Waterloo. He returned to Australia in 1823. (See note 120.)

205   'Two Jonstones' (Johnstons), probably sons of George Johnston, soldier and New South Wales landowner. Johnston was in England from 1800 to 1802 and evidently left two of his sons there for their education. Coneley is not identified.

206   The Ashley family is not identified further.

207   Elizabeth Bass to George Bass, 19 October 1803, ZML MSS 6544, ML, Sydney.

to inquire after you, he seems much interested about you desired to be remembered, I ashure you it does [word obscured] please me a little, he may have it in his power one day or other to be your friend should you want it. Andrew White[204] the two Jonstones & Coneley[205] Dined with us on Sunday they all look remarkably well beg you will remembr them to their Parents and tell them they are very happy. Andrew was disapointed at not receiving a Letter from his Mother, he is much grown in perfect health & very Handsom it seems his Father has taken the care of him from us, but poor fellow were we not to see after him. he would be totaly neglected, as he has never inquired after him since the last Holidays, but he still considers this his home and will always find it so. Mr Cressy had been particularly attentive in calling for anything I might have to send, I told you in a former Letter his Mother has been Dead near two Years, Mr Ashley & family[206] live where they did when you left England. The Old Gentleman had has a Paraletick Stroke all join me in Love Adieu

Then Elizabeth's brave front gave way.

My George I have made you several Jars of Pickles, must they spoil or will you come and eat them Oh I wish you had them[207]

208 William Waterhouse to George Bass, 17 October 1803, ZML MSS 6544, ML, Sydney.
209 Philip Gidley King to Robert, Lord Hobart, 1 March 1804, *HRA*, vol. IV, ed. Frederick Watson, 1915, pp. 523–4.
210 Philip Gidley King to Robert, Lord Hobart, 20 December 1804, *HRA*, vol. IV, ed. Frederick Watson, 1915, p. 172.

Elizabeth's fear of a French invasion was well founded. The peace agreement reached by Britain and France at Amiens on 27 March 1802 had collapsed in May the following year. From 1803 France faced only Britain as its opponent and Britain's defeat required an invasion of England, evidently planned for the northern autumn or winter of 1803. Napoleon's preparations were extensive and well publicised. An army of 150,000 men was encamped at Boulogne on the French coast. Almost 2000 ships and boats were assembled between Brest and Antwerp. While some historians have interpreted Napoleon's invasion project as a ruse, a pretext for raising a large army actually intended for use on the European continent, the prospect of invasion was real enough for the English. On 17 October 1803 William Waterhouse wrote to Bass,

'we are in hourly expectation of an Invasion by the French...'[208] It was a letter Bass never received.

George Bass had been away from New South Wales for eight months when Elizabeth wrote her unhappy letters of October 1803. No particular concern was felt in Sydney at the time for Bass' absence, as he was known to have planned a long voyage. However, in March 1804, Governor King wrote to Lord Hobart, Secretary of State for War and the Colonies, 'After a twelve-months' absence he is not yet returned, which makes me apprehensive for his safety.'[209] By December King concluded 'there is no doubt some accident has occurred'.[210]

Aware of the additional months it took for a letter to reach England from New South Wales, the concern of

211 See Informe No. 06—2003–DAC/TA, Archivo General de la
     Nación, Lima, Peru, in Bibliography. Earlier enquiries made by
     historian George William Rusden and Spanish scholar Don
     Pascual de Gayangos (*c.* 1903) yielded no evidence.

Bass' family was even less immediate, but as another year lengthened, and there was a growing silence with neither word nor letter, Elizabeth's anxiety would have mounted into anguish. Wordless years followed, during which Elizabeth's father and brother Henry attempted to find and trace any possible lead as to George Bass' disappearance. There were rumours, speculation, but nothing real. Elizabeth refused to believe that George was gone. She resisted petitioning for a naval widow's pension for more than two years after she became eligible, and rejected with indignation a later offer of marriage. She was George Bass' 'little wife', awaiting his return.

What was the fate of George Bass and the little brig *Venus*? Over the years no word or trace was found at the locations he planned to visit—New Zealand's Dusky Sound or Tahiti's Matavai Bay. Nor have examinations of nineteenth-century records in Spain and Peru revealed anything with regard to a George Bass having reached South America.[211] There seems little doubt but that somewhere in a stormy Tasman Sea or in the enormity of the Pacific Ocean George Bass met with circumstances that defeated even his skill, courage, and determination to return to Elizabeth. As with countless other ships at sea, the *Venus* disappeared.

Financial difficulties evidently overwhelmed William Waterhouse. The family left its home in Piccadilly for Smith Square, Westminster, and at some point Elizabeth took lodgings of her own in nearby Marsham Street. Her brother Henry died in 1812, possibly from the effects of

THE LETTERS OF GEORGE & ELIZABETH BASS

alcoholism, and their mother, Susanna Waterhouse, died three years later. Perhaps Elizabeth's deepest grief came with the death in 1822 of her unfailingly devoted father, who was, as she wrote, 'always kind to me'. Elizabeth Bass died two years later on 23 June 1824. She was 56 years old, and had faithfully waited 21 years for the return from the sea of her husband, George Bass.

BIBLIOGRAPHY

Primary sources

Banks Papers, series 72.005, Mitchell Library, State Library of New South Wales, Sydney

Bass, George, 'Bass's Journal of the Whaleboat Voyage', in *Matthew Flinders' Narrative of His Voyage in the Schooner* Francis, *1798, Preceded and Followed by Notes on Flinders, Bass, the Wreck of the Sydney Cove, &c by Geoffrey Rawson*, ed. Geoffrey Rawson, Golden Cockerel Press, Great Britain, 1946

——'Journal describing Two-Fold Bay in New South Wales, Furneaux's Islands in Bass's Strait and the coasts and harbours of Van Dieman's Land. from notes made on board the colonial sloop *Norfolk* in 1798 and 1799' [ms copy], Mitchell Library, State Library of New South Wales, Sydney

Bass/Waterhouse Papers, ZML MSS 6544 [ZSafe 1/187], Mitchell Library, State Library of New South Wales, Sydney

Baudin, Nicholas, *The Journal of Post Captain Nicholas Baudin, Commander-in-Chief of the Corvettes* Géographe *and* Naturaliste, trans. Christine Cornell, Libraries Board of South Australia, 1974

Bishop, Charles, *The Journal and Letters of Captain Charles Bishop on the North-West Coast of America, in the Pacific and in New South Wales 1794–1799*, ed. Michael Roe, Hakluyt Society, London, 1967

Bonwick Transcripts, Mitchell and Dixson Libraries, State Library of New South Wales, Sydney

Caley, George, *Reflections on the Colony of New South Wales*, ed. J.E.B. Currey, Resources Study, Canberra, 1866

Chapman, Frederik Henry as, *Architectura Navalis Mercatoria*, Coles, London, 1971. From selected parts of the nineteenth-century translation by the Rev. James Inman of the (author's) *Tractat Om Skepps-Byggieret*, originally published as *Architectura Navalis Mercatoria*, Holmiae, 1768.

Collins, David, *An Account of the English Colony in New South Wales, with Remarks on the Dispositions, Customs, Manners, etc., of the Native Inhabitants of that country*, vols I and II, ed. Brian H. Fletcher, A.H. & A.W. Reed, Sydney, 1975

Cook, James, *An Account of a Voyage Round the World with a full Account of the Voyage of the Endeavour in the Year MDCCLXX along the East Coast of Australia, by Lieutenant James Cook, Commander of His Majesty's Bark* Endeavour, ed. D. Warrington Evans, W.R. Smith & Paterson, Brisbane, 1969

——*Captain Cook's Journal during His First Voyage Round the World made in H.M. Bark 'Endeavour' 1768–1771*, ed. W.J.L. Wharton, Eliot Stock, 1893; Facsimile Edition, 1968

——*The Journal of Captain James Cook, edited from his original manuscripts by J.C. Beaglehole*, Hakluyt Society, Cambridge University Press, Cambridge, 1955–1974

Cullen, Peter, 'Memoirs of Peter Cullen', in *Five Naval Journals 1789–1817*, ed. H.G. Thursfield, Navy Records Society, London, 1951

Flinders, Matthew, *Charts of Terra Australis or Australia, showing the Parts Explored between 1798–1803 by M. Flinders, Commander of H.M.S.* Investigator, G. & W. Nicols, London, 1814

——*Matthew Flinders' Narrative of His Voyage in the Schooner* Francis, *1798, Preceded and Followed by Notes on Flinders, Bass, the Wreck of the Sydney Cove, &c by Geoffrey Rawson*, ed. Geoffrey Rawson, Golden Cockerel Press, Great Britain, 1946

——*Matthew Flinders' Narrative of* Tom Thumb's *Cruise to Canoe Rivulet*, ed. Keith M. Bowden, Southern Historical Association, Brighton, Victoria, 1985

——*Observations on the Coasts of Van Diemen's Land, on Bass's Strait and its Islands, and on part of the coasts of New South Wales; intended to accompany the charts of the late discoveries in those countries,* John Nichols, London, 1801; Australiana Facsimile Editions No. 66, Libraries Board of South Australia, Adelaide, 1965

——*A Voyage to Terra Australis; undertaken for the Purpose of Completing the Discovery of that Vast Country, and Prosecuted in the Years 1801, 1802, and 1803, in His Majesty's Ship the* Investigator, *and Subsequently in the Armed Vessel* Porpoise *and* Cumberland Schooner, *with an Account of the Shipwreck of the* Porpoise, *Arrival of the* Cumberland *at Mauritius, and Imprisonment of the Commander during Six Years and a Half on that Island,* vol. 1, G. & W. Nicols, London, 1814; Australiana Facsimile Editions No. 37, Libraries Board of South Australia, Adelaide, 1966

Hamilton, George, *A Voyage Round the World in His Majesty's Frigate* Pandora, Hordern House, Sydney, 1998

Historical Records of Australia, Governors' Despatches to and from England, Series I, vols I, II, III, IV, V, ed. Frederick Watson, the Library Committee of the Commonwealth Parliament, Sydney, 1914–15

Historical Records of New South Wales, vols I, II, III, IV, ed. F.M. Bladen, Charles Potter Government Printer, Sydney, and vol. V, ed. F.M. Bladen, William Applegate Gullick, Government Printer, Sydney, 1892, 1893, 1895, 1896, 1897

King, Philip Gidley, *The Journal of Philip Gidley King: Lieutenant, R.N., 1787–1790,* eds Paul G. Fidlon and R.J. Ryan, Australian Documents Library, Sydney, 1980

Logs of HMS *Flirt, Gorgon, Fairy, Pomona, Vulcan, Shark, Druid and Reliance,* The National Archives (TNA): Public Record Office (PRO), Kew, Richmond, UK

Noah, William, *Voyage to Sydney in the Ship* Hillsborough *1798–1799 and a Description of the Colony,* Library of Australian History, Sydney, 1978

Paine, Daniel, *The Journal of Daniel Paine: 1794–1797, Together with Documents Illustrating the Beginning of Government Boat-Building and Timber-gathering in New South Wales, 1795–1804,* eds R.J.B.

Knight and Alan Frost, National Maritime Museum, Greenwich, England and Library of Australian History, Sydney, 1983

Péron, François, *A Voyage of Discovery to the Southern Hemisphere, Performed by the Order of the Emperor Napoleon, during the Years 1801, 1802, 1803, and 1804*, translated from the French, Marsh Walsh, North Melbourne, 1975

Péron, M.F., *Voyage de découvertes aux terres Australes, exécuté par ordre de Su Majesté l'Empereur et Roi, sur les corvettes le Géographe, le Naturaliste, et la goelette le Casuarina, pendant les années 1800, 1801, 1802, 1803 et 1804; publié par décret impérial, sous le ministère de M. de Champagny, et rédigé par M.F. Péron*, trans. Moreno Giovannoni, Tome premier, A Paris, De L'Impremerie impériale M.DCCC, VII, 1807–16, pp. 393–4

Rusden Collection, Trinity College, the University of Melbourne, Melbourne

Shillinglaw Papers, Australian Manuscript Collection, State Library of Victoria, Melbourne

Suttor, George, *Memoirs of George Suttor, F.L.S., Banksian Collector (1774–1859)*, ed. George Mackaness, D.S. Ford, Sydney, 1948

Secondary sources

Aplin, Graeme, ed., *A Difficult Infant: Sydney before Macquarie*, New South Wales University Press, Kensington, 1988

Arnold, Dana, *Rural urbanism: London landscapes in the early nineteenth century*, Manchester University Press, Manchester, 2005

Atkinson, Alan, *The Europeans in Australia: a History*, vol. 1, Oxford University Press, South Melbourne, 1997

Australian Dictionary of Biography, vol. 1, 1788–1850, eds A.G.L. Shaw and C.M.H. Clark, Melbourne University Press, Carlton, Victoria, 1966

Australian Encyclopaedia, The, editor-in-chief Alec H. Chisholm, Grolier Society, Sydney, 1965

Badger, Geoffrey, *The Explorers of the Pacific*, 2nd edn, Kangaroo Press, Kenthurst, New South Wales, 1996

Barclay, Glen, *A History of the Pacific from the Stone Age to the Present Day*, Sidgwick & Jackson, London, 1978

Barker, Anthony, *When Was That? Chronology of Australia*, John Ferguson, Surry Hills, New South Wales, 1988

Bassett, Marnie, *The Governor's Lady: Mrs. Philip Gidley King*, Melbourne University Press, Melbourne, 1961

Beaglehole, J.C., *The Exploration of the Pacific*, Stanford University Press, Stanford, California, 1966

Becke, Louis and Jeffrey, Walter, *The Naval Pioneers of Australia*, John Murray, London, 1899

Begg, A. Charles and Begg, Neil C., *Dusky Bay*, Whitcombe & Tombs, Christchurch, New Zealand, 1966; rev. edn, 1968

Bernier, Oliver, *The World in 1800*, John Wiley & Sons, New York, 2000

Besant, Walter, *London in the 19th Century*, A. & C. Black, London, 1909

Birchall, James, *England under the Revolution and the House of Hanover*, Simpkin Marshall & Co., London, 1876

Birmingham, John, *Leviathan*, Random House, Milsons Point, New South Wales, 2000

Blainey, Geoffrey, *The Tyranny of Distance—How Distance Shaped Australia's History*, rev. edn, Sun Books, Sydney, 1983

Boulton, William, *The amusements of old London; being a survey of the sports and pastimes, tea gardens and parks, playhouses and other diversions of the people of London from the 17th to the beginning of the 19th century*, B. Blom, New York, 1969

Bowden, Keith M., *George Bass: 1771–1803, His Discoveries, Romantic Life and Tragic Disappearance*, Oxford University Press, Melbourne, 1952

Brodsky, Isadore, *Bennelong Profile: Dreamtime Reveries of a Native of Sydney Cove*, University Co-operative Bookshop, Sydney, 1973

Brown, Anthony, *Ill-Starred Captains—Flinders and Baudin*, Crawford House, Adelaide, 2000

Bryant, Joseph, *Captain Matthew Flinders, R.N., his voyages, discoveries and fortunes*, The Epworth Press, London, 1928

Butlin, S.J., *Foundations of the Australian Monetary System 1788–1851*, Sydney University Press, Sydney, 1968

Cameron, Hector Charles, *Sir Joseph Banks*, Angus & Robertson, Sydney, 1952

Campbell, I.C., *Worlds Apart—A History of the Pacific Islands*, Canterbury University Press, Christchurch, New Zealand, 2003

Campbell, Leon G., *The Military and Society in Colonial Peru, 1750–1810*, American Philosophical Society, Philadelphia, 1978

Carter, Harold B., *Sir Joseph Banks 1743–1820*, British Museum (Natural History), London, 1988

Chancellor, E. Beresford, *The XVIIIth Century in London; An Account of Its Social Life and Arts*, B.T. Batsford, London, 1920

Clancy, Robert, *The Mapping of Terra Australis*, Universal Press, Macquarie Park, New South Wales, 1995

Clowes, William Laird, *The Royal Navy—A History—From the Earliest Times to the Present*, vol. 5, Sampson Low, Marston, London, 1900

Cobley, John, *Sydney Cove 1793–1795—The Spread of Settlement*, Angus & Robertson, Sydney, 1983

——*Sydney Cove 1795–1800—The Second Governor*, Angus & Robertson, North Ryde, New South Wales, 1986

Cole, Harry and Cole, Valda, *Mr. Bass's Western Port—The Whaleboat Voyage*, Hastings-Western Port Historical Society in conjunction with the South Eastern Historical Association, Hastings, Victoria, 1997

Colledge, J.J., *Ships of the Royal Navy: An Historical Index*, vol. 1, David & Charles, Newton Abbot, England, 1969

Cook, A.M., *An Australian Boston: A Forgotten Chapter of Local History*, The Church House, Boston, England, 1943

——*Lincolnshire Links with Australia*, Keyworth and Sons, Lincoln, 1951

Cridland, Frank, *The Story of Port Hacking, Cronulla and Sutherland Shire*, Angus & Robertson, Sydney, 1924

Cumpston, J.H.L., *The Inland Sea and the Great River—the Story of Australian Exploration*, Angus & Robertson, Sydney, 1964

Cumpston, J.S., *Shipping Arrivals and Departures Sydney, 1788–1825*, Roebuck Society, Canberra, 1977

Dalrymple, Alexander, *An Historical Collection of the Several Voyages and Discoveries in the South Pacific Ocean*, Nourse, London, 1770

Daniel, Hawthorne, *Islands of the Pacific*, G.P. Putnam's Sons, New York, 1843

Duffy, Michael, *Man of Honour, John Macarthur—Duellist, Rebel, Founding Father*, Macmillan, Sydney, 2003

Dugard, Martin, *Farther Than Any Man: the Rise and Fall of Captain James Cook*, Allen & Unwin, Sydney, 2003

Egan, Jack, *Buried Alive: Sydney 1788–92, Eyewitness accounts of a nation*, Allen & Unwin, St Leonards, New South Wales, 1999

Ehrman, John, *The Younger Pitt: the Reluctant Transition*, Constable, London, 1983

Eisler, William and Smith, Bernard, *Terra Australis, the Furthest Shore*, International Cultural Corporation of Australia, Sydney, 1988

Ellis, M.H., *John Macarthur*, Angus & Robertson, Sydney, 1978

Ellis, William, *Polynesian Researches, during a Residency of Nearly Six Years in the South Sea Islands; including descriptions of the natural history and scenery of the islands, with remarks on the history, mythology, traditions, government, arts, manners and customs of the inhabitants*, vol. 1, Dowsons of Pall Mall, London, 1967

Estensen, Miriam, *The Life of George Bass: Surgeon and Sailor of the Enlightenment*, Allen & Unwin, Sydney, 2005

Evans, Susanna, *Historic Sydney as Seen by its Early Artists*, Doubleday, Lane Cove, New South Wales, 1983

Fernández-Shaw, Carlos M., *España y Australia. Cinco Siglos de Historia; Spain and Australia. Five Centuries of History*, edición Alonso Ibarrola y Mercedes Palau, Dirección General de Relaciónes Culturales y Científicas, Ministerio de Asuntus Exteriores de España, Spain, n.d.

Findlay, Alexander George, *Directory for the Navigation of the South Pacific Ocean; with descriptions of its Coasts, Islands, etc.; from the Strait of Magalhaens to Panama, and those of New Zealand, Australia, etc.; Its winds, currents and passages*, 5th edn, Richard Holmes Laurie, London, 1884

Fisher, J.R., *Government and Society in Colonial Peru: the intendant system 1784–1814*, University of London, London, 1970

Fisher, Robin and Johnston, Hugh, *Captain James Cook and His Times*, Australian National University Press, Canberra, 1979

Flannery, Tim, *The Birth of Sydney*, Text Publishing, Melbourne, 1999

Flynn, Michael, *The Second Fleet: Britain's Grim Convict Armada of 1790*, Library of Australian History, Sydney, 1993

Fraser, Don, ed., *Sydney—from Settlement to City, An Engineering History of Sydney*, Engineers Australia Pty Ltd, Sydney, 1999

Fregosi, Paul, *Dreams of Empire: Napoleon and the First World War 1792–1815*, Hutchinson, Sydney, 1989

Frost, Alan, 'A Place of Exile—Norfolk Island', in *Journeys into History*, ed. Graeme Davidson, Weldon Russell, Willoughby, New South Wales, 1990

——*Botany Bay Mirages: Illusions of Australia's Convict Beginnings*, Melbourne University Press, Melbourne, 1995

——*The Voyage of the Endeavour: Captain Cook and the Discovery of the Great South Land*, Allen & Unwin, Sydney, 1998

Frost, Alan and Samson, Jane, eds, *Pacific Empires: Essays in Honour of Glyndwr Williams*, Melbourne University Press, Carlton South, Victoria, 1999

Garran, Andrew, ed., *Picturesque Atlas of Australia*, vols 1 and 2, Picturesque Atlas Publishing, Melbourne, 1886

Gascoigne, John, *The Enlightenment and the European Origins of Australia*, Cambridge University Press, Port Melbourne, Victoria, 2002

——*Joseph Banks and the English Enlightenment—Useful Knowledge and Polite Culture*, Cambridge University Press, Cambridge, 1994

Gershoy, Leo, *The French Revolution and Napoleon*, Appleton-Century-Crofts, New York, 1933

Gibbons, Tony, gen. ed., *The Encyclopedia of Ships*, Silverdale, Enderby, Leicester, 2001

Hainsworth, D.R., *The Sydney Traders: Simeon Lord and His Contemporaries 1788–1821*, Melbourne University Press, Melbourne, 1981

Harben, Henry, *A Dictionary of London, being notes topographical and historical relating to the streets and principal buildings in the city of London*, Herbert Jenkins, London, 1918

Hardy, John and Frost, Alan, eds, *European Voyaging towards Australia*, Australian Academy of the Humanities, Canberra, 1990

Hoare, Merval, *Norfolk Island—A Revised and Enlarged History 1774–1998*, 5th edn, Central Queensland University Press, Rockhampton, Queensland, 1999

Holmes, (Mrs) Basil, *The London Burial Grounds—Notes on their history from the earliest times to the present day*, T. Fisher Unwin, London, 1846

Horner, Frank, *The French Renaissance: Baudin in Australia 1801–1803*, Melbourne University Press, Melbourne, 1987

Howgego, Raymond John, *Encyclopaedia of Exploration to 1800*, Hordern House Rare Books, Potts Point, New South Wales, 2003

Hughson, David, *London; Being an Accurate History and Description of the British Metropolis and its Neighbourhood, to Thirty Miles Extent, from an Actual Perambulation*, J. Stratford, London, 1808

Hunter, Susan and Carter, Paul, *Terre Napoléon—Australia through French Eyes 1800–1804*, Historic Houses Trust of New South Wales in Association with Hordern House, Sydney, 1999

Ingleton, Geoffrey C., *Matthew Flinders: Navigator and Chartmaker*, Genesis Publications, Guildford, Surrey, in association with Hedley Australia, Alphington, Victoria, 1986

James, William, *The Naval History of Great Britain from the Declaration of War by France in 1793 to the Accession of George IV*, vol. 1, Macmillan, New York, 1902

Jardine, Lisa, *Ingenious Pursuits: Building the Scientific Revolution*, Little, Brown & Co., London, 1999

Johnson, Nichola, *Eighteenth Century London*, Board of Governors of the Museum of London, London, 1991

Kelly's Directory of Lincolnshire 1905, Kelly's Directories, Ltd, London, 1905

Keneally, Tom, *The Commonwealth of Thieves—The Sydney Experiment*, Random House, Milsons Point, New South Wales, 2005

Kenny, John, *Before the First Fleet—The European Discovery of Australia 1606–1777*, Kangaroo Press, Kenthurst, New South Wales, 1995

King, Jonathan and King, John, *Philip Gidley King, A Biography of the Third Governor of New South Wales*, Methuen Australia, North Ryde, New South Wales, 1981

King, Robert J., *The Secret History of the Convict Colony: Alexandro Malaspina's Report on the British Settlement of New South Wales*, Allen & Unwin, Sydney, 1990

Kiple, Kenneth, *Plague, Pox and Pestilence, Diseases in History*, Phoenix, London, 1999

Lavery, Brian, *Nelson's Navy—The Ships, Men and Organisation 1793–1815*, Conway Maritime Press, London, 1989
——*Shipboard Life and Organisation 1731–1815*, Ashgate Publishing, Aldershot, England, 1998
Lee, Stephen J., *Aspects of European History 1494–1789*, 2nd edn, Routledge, London, 1984
Lewis, Michael, *The History of the British Navy*, Penguin, Harmondsworth, 1957
——*The Navy of Great Britain—A Historical Portrait*, George Allen & Unwin, London, 1948
——*A Social History of the Navy*, George Allen & Unwin, London, 1960
Lloyd, Christopher and Coulter, Jack L.S., *Medicine and the Navy—1200–1900*, vol. IV, 1815–1900, E. & S. Livingston, Edinburgh, 1963
Lyte, Charles, *Sir Joseph Banks—18th Century Explorer, Botanist and Entrepreneur*, A.H. & A.W. Reed, Sydney, 1980
MacDonald, Barrie, *Cinderellas of the Empire—Towards a History of Kiribati and Tuvalu*, Australian National University Press, Canberra, 1982
McDonald, W.G., *The First-Footers—Bass and Flinders in Illawarra—1796–1797*, Illawarra Historical Society, Wollongong, New South Wales, 1975
Mackaness, George, *Sir Joseph Banks—His Relations with Australia*, Angus & Robertson, Sydney, 1936
Mackesy, Piers, *War without Victory—The Downfall of Pitt 1799–1802*, Clarendon Press, Oxford, 1984
Maiden, J.H., *Sir Joseph Banks—The 'Father of Australia'*, William Applegate Gullick, Sydney, 1909
Marcus, G.J., *A Naval History of England: The Age of Nelson*, George Allen & Unwin, London, 1948
Masefield, John, *Sea Life in Nelson's Time*, 3rd edn, Conway Maritime Press, London, 1971
Maurois, André, *A History of England*, The Bodley Head, London, 1956
Mee, Arthur, ed., *The King's England: Lincolnshire, A County of Infinite Charm*, Hodder & Stoughton, London, 1949

Miller, David Philip and Reill, Peter Hanns, eds, *Visions of Empire: Voyages, Botany and Representations of Nature*, Cambridge University Press, Cambridge, 1996

Miller, Nathan, *Broadsides—The Age of Fighting Sail, 1775–1815*, John Wiley & Sons, New York, 2000

Morris, Kenneth, *George Bass in Western Port, Incorporating George Bass and the Convicts*, Bass Valley Historical Society, Victoria, 1997

Morris, Roger, ed., *The Channel Fleet and the Blockade of Brest 1793–1801*, Ashgate for the Navy Records Society, Aldershot, England, 2000

Mountfort, Pam, *Despatches, Departures and Undesirables in Early New South Wales*, Books and Writers Network, Watsons Bay, New South Wales, 2005

Mourot, Suzanne, *This Was Sydney—A Pictorial History from 1788 to the Present*, Ure Smith, Sydney, 1969

Nicholson, Ian, *Log of Logs; A catalogue of logs, journals, shipboard diaries, letters, and all forms of voyage narratives, 1788–1988, for Australia and New Zealand, and surrounding oceans*, Roebuck Society No. 41, published by the author jointly with the Australian Association for Maritime History, Nambour, Queensland, n.d.

O'Brian, Patrick, *Joseph Banks—A Life*, Collins Narvill, London, 1987

Perry, T.M., *The Discovery of Australia—The Charts and Maps of the Navigators and Explorers*, Nelson, Melbourne, 1982

Peters, Merle, *The Bankstown Story—A Comprehensive History of the District*, published by the author, Yagoona, 1969

Pope, Steve, *Hornblower's Navy—Life at Sea in the Age of Nelson*, Orion, London, 1998

Proudfoot, Helen, Bickford, Anne, Egloff, Brian, Stocks, Robin, *Australia's First Government House*, Allen & Unwin, Sydney, 1991

Radok, Rainer, *Capes and Captains—A Comprehensive Study of the Australian Coast*, Surrey Beaty & Sons, Chipping Norton, New South Wales, 1990

Reader's Digest Guide to the Australian Coast, Reader's Digest Services, Surry Hills, New South Wales, 1983

Rebeiro, Aileen, *The Art of Dress: Fashion in England and France 1750 to 1820*, Yale University Press, New Haven, 1995

Ross, John, editor-in-chief, *Chronicle of Australia*, Viking, Penguin Books Australia, Ringwood, Victoria, 2000

Rusden, G.W., *Curiosities of Colonization*, Chapter V, (no publisher), London, 1874, pp. 16–38

——*History of Australia*, vol. 1, Melville, Mullen & Slade, Melbourne, 1897

Sailing Directions (Enroute) for the Pacific Islands, Defence Mapping Agency and Hydrographic/Topographic Center, Washington, D.C., 1982

Scott, Ernest, *The Life of Captain Matthew Flinders, R.N.*, Angus & Robertson, Sydney, 1914

Shaw, A.G.L., and Clark, C.M.H., eds, *Australian Dictionary of Biography, 1788–1850*, vols 1 and 2, Melbourne University Press, Melbourne, 1966

Sidney, Samuel, *The Land of the Kangaroo and the Boomerang: also giving a true history of the discovery, settlement and wonderful growth of the Australian colonies*, Hurst & Co., New York, 1880

Skelton, R.A., *Explorers' Maps—Chapters in the Cartographic Record of Geographical Discovery*, Routledge and Kegan Paul, London, 1958

Smith, Bernard, *Imagining the Pacific—In the Wake of the Cook Voyages*, Miegunyah Press, Carlton South, Victoria, 1992

Soper, Tony, *The National Trust Guide to the Coast*, Webb & Bower, Exeter, 1984

Stephensen, P.R. and Kennedy, Brian, *The History and Description of Sydney Harbour*, A.H. & A.W. Reed, Sydney, 1980

Storey, Edward, *Spirit of the Fens, A View of Fenland Life Past and Present*, Robert Hale, London, 1985

Summerson, John, *Georgian London*, Borne & Jenkins, London, 1988

Taylor, Peter, *Australia—The First Twelve Years*, George Allen & Unwin, Sydney, 1982

Thompson, Pishey, *The History and Antiquities of Boston, and the Villages of Skirbeck, Fishtoft, Frelston, Butterwick, Benington, Leverton, Leake, and Wrangle; Comprising the Hundred of Skirbeck in the County of Lincoln*, John Noble, Jun., Boston, England, 1856

Tooley, Ronald Vere, *Maps and Map-Makers*, Batsford, London, 1952

——*Tooley's Dictionary of Mapmakers*, Map Collector Publications, Tring, 1979

Walsh, Michael and Yallop, Colin, eds, *Language and Culture in Aboriginal Australia*, Aboriginal Studies Press, Canberra, 1993

Watt, James, 'The Colony's Health', in *Studies from Terra Australis to Australia*, eds John Hardy and Alan Frost, Australian Academy of the Humanities, Canberra, 1989

——'The Health of Sailors', in *European Voyaging towards Australia*, eds John Hardy and Alan Frost, Australian Academy of the Humanities, Canberra, 1990

Watt, J., Freeman, E.J. and Bynum, W.F., eds, *Starving Sailors—The Influence of Nutrition upon Naval and Maritime History*, National Maritime Museum, Greenwich, 1981

Way, Thomas R. and Bell, Walter G., *The Thames from Chelsea to the Nore*, John Lane, The Bodley Head, London, 1907

Weinreb, Ben and Hibbert, Christopher, eds, *The London Encyclopaedia*, Macmillan, London, 1983

Williams, Glyndwr and Frost, Alan, eds, *Terra Australis to Australia*, Oxford University Press, Melbourne, 1988

Wills, Geoffrey, *The English Life Series—c. 1760–1820, George III*, vol. IV, Wheaton, Exeter, 1968

Wright, Thomas, *England under the House of Hanover*, vols 1 and 2, Richard Bentley, London, 1848

Articles

Andrews, Alan E.J., 'Mount Hunter and Beyond: with Hunter, Bass, Tench, Wilson, Barrallier, Caley, King, and Macquarie, 1790–1815', *Journal of the Royal Australian Historical Society*, vol. 76, no. 1, pp. 3–15

Bowden, K.M., 'George Bass, 1771–1803, Surgeon and Sailor', *Bulletin of the Post-Graduate Committee in Medicine, University of Sydney*, vol. 17, May 1961

Coleman, Edith, 'George Bass, Victoria's First Explorer and Naturalist', *Victorian Naturalist*, vol. 67, 1950, pp. 3–9

Cook, A.M., 'Men of Lincoln Who Sailed with Cook', *Royal Australian Historical Society Journal and Proceedings*, vol. 35, Part 2, Sydney, 1949

Doughty, Oswald, 'The English Malady of the Eighteenth Century', *The Review of English Studies*, vol. II, no. 7, July 1926

Else-Mitchell, R., 'Bass's Land Explorations', *Royal Historical Society Journal and Proceedings*, vol. xxxvii, Part iv, Sydney, 1951

Graves, Kathleen E., 'The Distant Climate and Savage Shore—Being the Life of George Bass', *Walkabout—Australian Geographical Magazine*, 1 August 1957, pp. 10–14

Norrie, H., 'Australia's Debt to Her Early Medicos', *Sydney University Medical Journal*, July 1933, vol. XXVII, Part I, pp. 136–43

Parsons, T.G., 'Was John Boston's Pig a Political Radical? The Reaction to Popular Radicalism in New South Wales', *Journal of the Royal Australian Historical Society*, vol. 71, Part 5, 1986, pp. 163–77

Roe, Michael, 'Australia's Place in the "Swing to the East" 1788–1810', *Historical Studies—Australia and New Zealand*, vol. 8, November 1957–May 1959, pp. 202–13

——'Colonial Society in Embryo', *Historical Studies: Australia and New Zealand*, vol. 7, November 1955–May 1957, pp. 149–59

——'New Light on George Bass, Entrepreneur and Intellectual', *Journal of the Royal Australian Historical Society*, vol. 72, Part 5, 1987, pp. 251–73

Scott, Ernest, 'The Early History of Western Port—Part I', *The Victorian Historical Magazine*, vol. 6, no. 1, September 1917, pp. 1–4

Miscellaneous

Fitzgerald, Lawrence, 'Bass's "Barmouth Creek"', address given at Tathra, New South Wales, to the Tathra Historical Society, 3 June 1976

Informe No. 06—2003–DAC/TA, Archivo General de la Nación, Lima, Peru

Letter by 'Oceanus', *The Naval Chronicle for 1813 Containing a General and Biographical History of The Royal Navy of the United Kingdom; with a Variety of Original Papers on Nautical Subjects*, vol. XXX, Joyce Gold, London, 1813, p. 201

List of Those Examined and Approved Surgeons, July 1789, The Corporation of Surgeons of London, Private Collection of William F. Wilson, Melbourne and 'Bass River', Victoria

The Sydney Gazette and New South Wales Advertiser, Facsimile Reproductions, vols 1, 2, 3, 6 and 7, The Trustees of the Public Library of New South Wales in Association with Angus & Robertson, Sydney, 1964, 1966, 1969